MW00679649

The Integrated Approach to Student Achievement

A results-driven model for improving performance, leadership, and the culture of instruction at your school

The Integrated Approach to Student Achievement: A results-driven model for improving performance, leadership, and the culture of instruction at your school
Donyall D. Dickey
  140 pp.
  References pp. 121–122

© 2010 Donyall D. Dickey
Published by aha! Process, Inc.

All rights reserved. No part of this book may be reproduced in any manner whatsoever without written permission, except in the case of brief quotations embedded in critical articles and reviews. For information, contact:

aha! Process, Inc.
P.O. Box 727
Highlands, TX 77562-0727
(800) 424-9484 ▪ (281) 426-5300
Fax: (281) 426-5600
Website: www.ahaprocess.com

Library of Congress Control Number: 2009939769
  ISBN 13: 978-1-934583-39-5
  ISBN 10: 1-934583-39-1

Copy editing by Marianne Taflinger and Dan Shenk
Book design by Paula Nicolella
Cover design by Naylor Design

Printed in the United States of America

The Integrated Approach to Student Achievement

A results-driven model for improving performance, leadership, and the culture of instruction at your school

Donyall D. Dickey

TABLE OF CONTENTS

Acknowledgments   vii

Foreword   ix

Chapter One   1
Addressing Lowered Expectations

Chapter Two   11
Establishing a Culture of Instruction

Chapter Three   35
Establishing the Imperative—
Examine the Data

Chapter Four   43
Analyzing the Demands of the
State Curriculum

Chapter Five   77
Developing an Action Plan for the
Tested Areas

Chapter Six   87
Reporting the Progress

Chapter Seven   97
Composing Higher Order Objectives

Chapter Eight   107
Planning Explicit Instruction

Appendix A   113
Integrated Approach: Professional
Development Seminars

Appendix B   115
Integrated Approach: Informal
Observation Checklist

Appendix C   117
Integrated Approach to Student
Achievement Implementation Rubric

References   121

Index   123

About the Author   129

ACKNOWLEDGMENTS

Writing this book has been the fulfillment of a lifelong dream. It represents a nexus of my work as a teacher, instructional leader, school administrator, and advocate for rigorous, targeted instruction for all children from all backgrounds. I wrote this book while running a middle school, writing a doctoral dissertation, and conducting professional development workshops on this approach across the country. What kept me writing day and night was the notion that this book could equip a learning community battling the scourge of underperformance with the tools necessary to achieve success for children and their families.

I know all too well that a quality education is one of the keys to opening doors that might otherwise have remained closed, so it is a privilege to share this approach to instructional leadership with my honorable colleagues in the profession. Our work is noble because it helps to build and rebuild the foundation of our society: the minds of our young people.

I would like to thank three talented educators for their encouragement: Linda Wise, Becky Kaatz, and Dr. Ruby Payne. A special thank you goes to my dear friends and "cheerleaders"— Steaven Hamlin, Kevin Mohorn, Calvin Green, Christel Perry, Jewel Benford, and Leroy Bazzle, all of whom provided me with unique and genuine support.

Most importantly, I would like to acknowledge the students who have afforded me the honor of being their mentor, advocate, and principal.

–Donyall Dickey

FOREWORD

During a trip back home two years ago, I was given an opportunity to have coffee with a gentleman who, I was told, possessed information and an instructional approach that was needed to advance student achievement in my new school. Before becoming principal of this particular school, I had worked only in schools that took a "nudge or a tweak," and scores would improve. Just recently, however, I moved to a school that needed a complete overhaul.

When first approached about this meeting, I was reluctant to seek assistance or to listen to one more "new" educational innovation or program. As a seasoned principal, my staff and I had always attained AYP (adequate yearly progress). I kept telling myself that I was going to have the same success at my new school, but in my heart I knew what I had always done would not be enough.

So we met at the coffee shop in order for me to listen to yet another idea on how to save children and meet AYP. This charismatic and dynamic individual shared a new approach with me, using examples and results—and convincing me that it was the only way to make a difference with kids. But this approach was, at first, so overwhelming that I could not quite embrace it. Although the entire process was clear and made sense, how could I take what he said and change the school culture of instruction? All the way home I pondered his words and could not let go of his concept of helping all students reach the standard of achievement. For our school, it meant all students would meet or exceed the state standard as measured by performance on the annual standardized assessment in the spring, a truly audacious goal.

After meeting with my staff, we decided to dive into implementing the approach, so I invited my newfound friend, Donyall Dickey, to train the faculty. He presented the Integrated Approach, and we soon began our journey. He helped us to align our state curriculum with our county's curriculum, identify core prerequisite skills for student achievement in reading and mathematics, and adopt unique methods for teaching and reteaching in an intentional and systematic way. The results were quickly apparent in our weekly pre-test/post-test results, and students soon owned and applied what they learned.

The information presented here will give you an opportunity to read, reflect, and hopefully apply these principles to achieve success with all students. Our students took the state test after less than a year of working with Donyall and achieved a total of 48% growth in reading and math—24% in each area. We have much work to still do but will rely on the adoption of the Integrated Approach to continue our journey.

–Jacqueline S. Conarton, Ph.D.
Principal
Goldfarb Elementary School
Las Vegas, Nevada

CHAPTER ONE

Addressing Lowered Expectations

> *"Lowered expectations are dangerous and counterproductive to promoting student achievement."*

One of the greatest catalysts of increased student achievement is high teacher expectations. Brown and Medway (2007) conducted a case study examining the impact of school climate and teacher beliefs on student achievement in a school serving primarily poor minority students. The researchers found that high teacher expectations, regardless of student background, promoted academic achievement (as measured by performance on state-mandated assessments in language arts, mathematics, and science), even among previously underperforming student groups and individuals. Brown and Medway also found that the teachers studied in this school uniformly reported that they expected all of their students to learn and communicated high expectations daily, beginning with the first day of school. For students who were victims of low self-expectations and previous academic failures, the teachers worked actively to change students' beliefs about their personal abilities in order to make academic gains. The end result of the teachers' efforts and expectations was increased student achievement as measured by performance on standardized assessments.

As teachers and school leaders, we must recognize the power of expectations and actively challenge both our preconceived notions of our students and assist them in developing healthy self-expectations. Lowered teacher expectations are just as damaging to student achievement and school improvement as high expectations are helpful. Lowered teacher expectations manifest themselves in: (a) poor planning; (b) rote memory tasks or activities that require students to regurgitate information exactly as presented by the teacher; and (c) an absence of routine reflective practices at the close of a lesson, unit, quarter, and/or semester.

Lowered expectations, as expressed through poor planning, are made evident by an absence of, and in some cases, an individual's reluctance to compose daily lesson plans. How can one facilitate sound, thoughtful instruction without a plan? Research suggests that a student taught by an ineffective teacher for one year (in any content area) needs two consecutive years of sound instruction to reach grade level. Furthermore, a student taught by an ineffective teacher for two consecutive years never fully recovers in that content area. Teaching without a lesson plan is equivalent to driving from coast to coast in the United States without a roadmap; you might get to your destination eventually, but not without a significant number of needless wrong turns.

WITHOUT A LESSON PLAN, HOW DOES A TEACHER ...

- Consider the formal materials of instruction?

- Incorporate prior knowledge (the prerequisite for new learning)?

- Introduce unfamiliar words and concepts in the content to be taught?

- Model skills to be acquired?

- Place formative assessments strategically throughout the lesson, including cooperative practice opportunities which allow for peer coaching?

- Formulate independent assessments to drive subsequent instructional decisions?

I'm strongly convinced that if we, as teachers and school leaders, insisted that teaching in our classrooms and schools were representative of the quality of daily instruction that we want for our own offspring, millions of children would have little or no difficulty demonstrating adequate yearly progress (AYP). Passing a basic skills state assessment in reading/English and mathematics should not be as complicated and difficult as it has become. These tests are written below grade level and represent the bottom of the instructional bucket. Student achievement is simplistic; it is a matter of input and output. If students are taught to mastery by teachers who believe in their ability to achieve, these children, whom we thought could not achieve at high levels, will not only meet our expectations but will exceed them. What I just stated may sound strong—and may contradict some schools of thought—but for the sake of the children who sit in classrooms receiving poor instruction from one year to the next entering middle school reading two or three grade levels below the standard or entering high school reading at a sixth-grade level (which is common for poor and minority students in this nation), I emphatically argue its truth. To educators and advocates who promote excellence in teaching and learning, teaching (or allowing others to teach) without a lesson plan is malpractice.

Using rote memory tasks in instruction was common 20 years ago and widely regarded as acceptable, but the world has changed dramatically and so, too, must the instruction—in order that children may compete in an evolving, global society. Memorizing content-related facts certainly has its place in the classroom. Students should know basic facts about science, history, English (rules for grammar, mechanics, and syntax), and mathematical concepts, but basic facts alone are not sufficient. Instruction that merely requires students to regurgitate facts without also requiring them to apply that knowledge, analyze it (take it apart) and synthesize it (put it back together in a new way), evaluate (make judgments), and create new constructs and understanding of facts and concepts, is not instruction at all. I would suggest that it falls profoundly short of the standard that our students (regardless of race, ethnicity, socioeconomic status, limited English proficiency, or disability) deserve and which taxpayers should be able to expect from our public schools.

Furthermore, when did "rigor" become a bad word? A lack of instructional rigor on a daily basis is the adversary of student achievement and school improvement. Thousands and thousands of students and schools across the nation are failing the state-mandated basic skills exam. Why? I see the answer plainly when I train (K–12) instructional leaders and teachers at all stages in the school-improvement process. Many students are receiving instruction that does not require them to do anything with what they know. Students should receive instruction that imposes increasing cognitive demands, not instruction which rewards regurgitation of facts, completion of worksheets (e.g., dittos), or word-find puzzles. Instruction that is characterized by high teacher expectations guarantees opportunities for students to grapple with the content and concepts for the purpose of building critical-thinking, problem-solving skills.

In my tenure as a teacher and school leader, the most effective teachers have not necessarily been those who earned degrees from the most prestigious institutions or those who have come from a lineage of educators, but those who have valued personal reflection as a tool for continuously improving their classroom instruction. A teacher who is reflective is demonstrating a concern for all her or his learners by reflecting:

- How did my thoughts about the content/concept impede or stimulate student acquisition of new skills/knowledge?

- Did I clear up misconceptions related to the content/concepts that could have blocked student acquisition of new skills/knowledge?

- Do I need to reteach the content/concept?

- What resources are available to me to better understand and teach the content/concept, and how do I access them?

I have found that teachers who don't reflect on their practices are teachers who are likely to be more concerned with assessments than with teaching students to the threshold of mastery.

Lisa Delpit (2006) suggests that lowered teacher expectations is a deadly fog formed when the cold mist of bias and ignorance meets the warm, vital reality of children of color in many of our schools. I agree with her assertion but believe that it is incomplete. I would argue that lowered teacher expectations are more like carbon monoxide—an invisible, largely silent threat to the academic success of not only children of color, but also an ever-present threat to the academic success of all children reared in low-income households, students receiving special education, English language learners (ELL), and those without involved parents. Every day, across this nation, academic expectations are set for children based upon their ZIP code, how they look, and our preconceived notions of their abilities. This practice is wrong, and it has a lasting impact on both the quantity and quality of instruction that they receive over the course of their K–12 academic career.

So, let's be realistic; no one will stand up in a faculty meeting to voluntarily expose himself as one who harbors lowered expectations for certain groups of students. It will not happen that way. However, conversations in the teachers' lounge, team meetings, and the parking lot will provide insight into this silent threat to student achievement and school improvement called lowered expectations. School and teacher leaders must be responsive to these conversations in order to address the harmful behaviors that result from such biases. In fact, schools that are designated as "failing" by the state's standard already have enough naysayers and critics on the sidelines unaware of how hard some teachers and administrators are working in such a school to "turn it around." What a school community under this extraordinary pressure does not need are people on the staff who privately doubt the student's ability to perform on grade level or beyond. As the old adage suggests, "A house divided against itself cannot stand."

Lowered teacher expectation is a pervasive issue facing students in low-performing schools and selected groups of students in high-performing schools; therefore, it must be addressed directly by the instructional leader (principal) and reinforced by each member of the site-based administrative team, including the assistant principal(s)—who could at any moment become a principal, department chairs (content leaders), and grade-level team leaders in elementary and middle schools. Lowered expectations have no place in a learning community committed to establishing a culture of instruction designed to assist the process of effective, reflective teaching, and enduring learning. Goddard, Hoy, and Hoy (2000) agree, calling for collective efficacy, which is defined as the "perceptions of teachers in a school that the efforts of the faculty as a whole will have a positive effect on students and that such efficacy can be more important than socioeconomic status in explaining a school's achievement level."

As you will see in the chapters to follow, this approach to instruction is built on the premise and precept that all students— regardless of race, ethnicity, socioeconomic status, English language proficiency, or disability—will outperform common expectations when consistently exposed to high-quality, targeted instruction planned and delivered by teachers who genuinely believe in students' innate ability to achieve.

Figure 1.1—Theory of Peak Performance

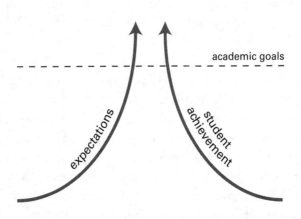

Expectations and Student Achievement

NOTE. Students who are aware of the high expectations set for them by their teachers will not only meet academic goals set for them, in many instances they will exceed them.

Although the discussion in this chapter was somewhat limited to a discussion of lowered teacher expectations, the academic and behavioral expectations of all adults who have daily access to students must be examined and addressed systematically. For planning purposes, the chart below will prove useful to identifying and developing a plan of action for teachers, teacher assistants, administrators, and support staff. Site-based teams can use it to assess expectations, identify evidence of lowered expectations, and formulate possible responses and/or professional development opportunities for groups and individuals.

Table 1.1 — Lowered Expectations Action Template

Evidence of Lowered Expectations as Demonstrated by Administration	Improvement Plan of Action
Evidence of Lowered Expectations as Demonstrated by Teachers	Improvement Plan of Action
Evidence of Lowered Expectations as Demonstrated by Instructional Assistants	Improvement Plan of Action
Evidence of Lowered Expectations as Demonstrated by Support Staff	Improvement Plan of Action

NOTE: Use this template with your leadership team to identify the attitudes, beliefs, and behaviors that are counterproductive to student achievement and school improvement that sometimes go underaddressed or unaddressed all together. Formulate a plan of action for each group represented on the table and plan to communicate a plan for holding members of each group accountable.

CHAPTER TWO

Establishing a Culture of Instruction

> *"All learning communities have a culture, many articulate meaningful and measurable instructional goals, but few have a culture of instruction."*

Of which of the following cultural groups are you a member: American Indian, Jewish, Italian, Polish, African-American, Spanish, or Irish? If you are not a member of one of these groups, you undoubtedly are a member of some larger group. We all are. Here's my point: As a member of a cultural group, you are fully aware of its tenets, even if you choose not to subscribe to them. For instance, the vast majority of people of Irish descent practice Catholicism; Italians are likely tell you that their mothers are extremely nurturing; and African Americans almost always refer to close friends of the family as cousins, though they are not related biologically. Members of cultural groups have insider knowledge of norms and taboos unique to the group.

In another example, if I were a Native American, it is very likely that I would have intimate knowledge of the traditions of my people, and I might be an expert on the themes and structures of the stories told by my forefathers. I may also have profound knowledge of the history of my people, and I would expect others in my community to have similar knowledge and ability to converse on topics related to shared values, ideas, and practices. Moreover, I would expect the mature members of my community to teach the immature, in an effort to keep valuable traditions alive, even after the patriarch or matriarch dies.

So why is it that when I walk through schools or facilitate professional development workshops and ask teachers and instructional leaders to describe their culture of instruction, I get as many answers as the number of people asked? No two people agree on a description of their schoolwide culture of instruction, yet every day children are blamed for their underperformance—when in many instances it's the lack of an agreed-upon culture of instruction (among the adults) that has a greater impact on underachievement than demographics ever could. In fact, I do not believe that the ZIP code of a student's neighborhood should be a predictor of individual student performance; rather the quality of instruction "in the neighborhood school" should be the leading predictor of student performance. Allow me to pose another rhetorical question.

WHAT IS THE CULTURE OF INSTRUCTION IN YOUR BUILDING/SYSTEM?

Now, I am not asking you to describe your reading or mathematics intervention; nor am I asking you to describe the overpriced textbooks you hoped would be the panacea for lackluster teaching; nor am I even asking you to recite your school's vision statement (you know ... the one that no one really knows). What I am asking, however, is what are the theories (body of rules, ideas, principles, and techniques) that underpin pedagogy (the science of teaching and learning) in your school/school system? If you cannot answer this question, the members of your staff may be "all talk." While this may be no fault of their own, they may be using the language of collaboration without actually living it. Peel back the surface of rhetoric; you might be astonished by what you find.

If your school has not asked itself this question (What is our culture of instruction?), and your students are meeting with academic success, I fear the following may be taking place: (a) Your school has demographics working in its favor, and/or (b) your student body is achieving in spite of your leadership. If your school is underachieving, you cannot expect it to become a higher achieving school when the members of your school culture (administrators, teachers, and support staff) operate in the absence of a mutually agreed upon set of values, ideas, and practices. Even if your underachieving school experiences an abrupt spike in student achievement, such gains will be unsustainable if savvy members of the learning community have an inability to teach and integrate new members into the values, beliefs, and behaviors of the school's culture of instruction that created its success.

To establish a culture of instruction conducive to student achievement and school improvement, schools and school systems must address four major considerations: (1) instructional theory, (2) instructional imperatives, (3) data analysis, and (4) administrative support. The answers to the following culture of instruction consideration questions will serve as the basis for formulating site-based common beliefs, instructional practices, data protocols, and administrative supports vital for building individual capacity, fostering a culture of collaboration and shared decision making, and promoting sustained student achievement and school improvement.

Table 2.1—Culture of Instruction Quadrants
(Componentsand Considerations)

I.	**Instructional Theory:** What does the research (body of literature) in the field suggest are the most effective rules, ideas, principles, and techniques for promoting student achievement, particularly if they are distinct from current ways of thinking?
II.	**Instructional Imperatives:** What are the schoolwide instructional practices that promote student achievement and school improvement?
III.	**Data Analysis:** What information (data) should be collected and by whom? To whom should the data be reported? How frequently should the data be reported? How should the data be reported? In what settings should the data be reported?
IV.	**Administrative Support:** How does the site-based administrative team provide targeted and consistent support for teachers and staff to mitigate or remove obstacles to student achievement and school improvement?

Figure 2.1—Culture of Instruction Quadrants
(Components and Considerations)

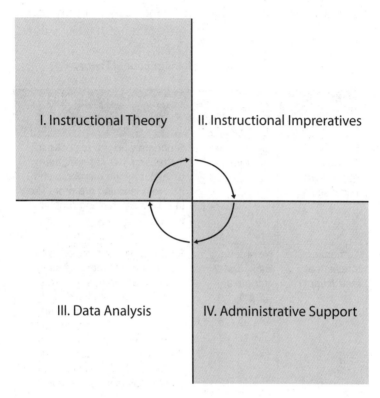

NOTE: *The interaction of the four quadrants produces learning communities that are able to lift the tide of instruction for all students, driving student achievement and school improvement.*

Below are research-driven or action-research based definitions and examples for each of the four quadrants of the Integrated Approach for Student Achievement and School Improvement.

Table 2.2—Quadrant I: Instructional Theory

Integrated Approach Component	Theorist	Research-Based Description
Cognitive Pluralism/ Higher Order Thinking	Eisner (1979) and Bloom (1956)	Students who are exposed to instruction that requires them to think beyond memorization and rote learning are more likely to be critical-thinking problem solvers.
Authentic Intellectual Instruction	Newmann, Byrk, and Nagoaka (2001)	Students who are exposed to instruction that requires them to apply, analyze, and create in a rigorous way achieve at high levels, earning standardized test scores 20% higher than the national average, outperforming their unexposed peers by as much as 32 points in reading and 48 points in mathematics.

CHAPTER TWO: ESTABLISHING A CULTURE OF INSTRUCTION

Table 2.2—Quadrant I: Instructional Theory
(continued)

Integrated Approach Component	Theorist	Research-Based Description
Cooperative Learning and Small Group Instruction	Baker, (1999); Hudley (1997); Quinn (2002)	Cooperative learning—Students are intentionally placed by the teacher in learning cohorts to teach them responsibility for learning and peer coaching, through which each member of the group is held accountable for encouraging others to complete tasks and attain skills. Findings from numerous studies on the strategy suggest that ethnically and linguistically diverse students demonstrate significant academic gains, improved behavior and attendance, self-confidence and motivation, as well as school and classmates' satisfaction.
Co-Teaching	Wilson and Michaels (2006)	The researchers found that all students responded favorably to co-teaching by receiving better grades, developing improved literacy skills, and showing an interest in participating in co-taught classes in the future. Special education students reported that co-taught classes gave them the opportunity to gain access to the general curriculum. General education students reported that co-taught classes provided them the opportunity to be exposed to higher levels of abstraction, concept development, and skill development.

Table 2.2—Quadrant I: Instructional Theory
(continued)

Integrated Approach Component	Theorist	Research-Based Description
Guided Notes	Patterson (2005)	When minority and special education students were provided with partially completed notes, they overcame the challenge of simultaneously listening to the teacher lecture, processing information, deciding what was important, and recording important facts to remember.
Teacher Expectations	Fisher (2005)	The researcher found that the majority of teachers within a school had prejudged underachieving students prior to examining their individual academic strengths and weaknesses, which negatively impacted student performance.

Table 2.3—Quadrant II: Instructional Imperatives

Integrated Approach Component	Action-Research Description
Knowledge of State Curriculum	Each state, as required by federal mandates, has written and published a state curriculum for reading/English and mathematics for K–12, complete with standards/objectives/assessment limits to be tested in select grades in elementary, middle, and high school. This document must be your school's instructional starting point; it identifies the skills that will be invariably assessed by grade level and content area. This important document should be utilized to drive instructional decisions and can be found on your state department of education website (see Chapter 4). In the coming years, we should expect the individual state standards to be replaced by national standards for reading and mathematics, but they will not be radically different from current state standards, with the exception of mathematics standards, which will be reduced in number.
State Glossary for Reading and Mathematics	Each state also publishes (usually in the first few or last few pages of the state curriculum) core vocabulary words that students must understand to attain mastery-level knowledge of the content and demonstrate adequate yearly progress by meeting instructional standards. These core vocabulary words are used by your state to pose questions on the standardized assessment. If students do not understand the wording of assessment questions, they are unlikely to be able to respond appropriately.

Table 2.3—Quadrant II: Instructional Imperatives
(continued)

Integrated Approach Component	Action-Research Description
Action Plan for Explicitly Teaching Assessment Limits	Assessment limits are the most that will be assessed by the state and the least that should be taught in the classroom. To that end, schools should use the state curriculum to identify the skills to be assessed, and develop a plan of action to explicitly instruct all students on the standards/objective/ assessment limits to be assessed by grade level for reading/English and mathematics by grade level, across the content areas. (See Chapter 5.)
Performance-Based Objectives	For optimal results, objectives should be composed in the "content-related KNOW" and "higher order DO" format. "KNOW and DO" objectives are performance-based objectives that are one part content and one part higher order thinking. Performance-based objectives honor your system's essential curriculum and recognize the importance of requiring students to "do something" with what they have learned. (See Chapter 7.)

Table 2.3—Quadrant II: Instructional Imperatives
(continued)

Integrated Approach Component	Action-Research Description
Explicit Instruction Lesson Plan Format	Each school system subscribes to its own "Essential Curriculum," the curriculum that all are instructed to know and teach. The skills identified in your system's essential curriculum include those that will be assessed on your state assessment. While embedded there for students who traditionally underperform, these skills must be taught more explicitly. Integrated Approach lessons: • Provide students with an explicit teacher model (think aloud). • Include a teacher lead (where students lead the teacher by thinking out loud to demonstrate their developing understanding of the concept/content). • Allow for cooperative learning opportunities in which students have to work collaboratively in small groups to perform the same task. • End with an independent test that requires each student to demonstrate individual skill attainment. (See Chapter 8.)

Table 2.3—Quadrant II: Instructional Imperatives
(continued)

Integrated Approach Component	Action-Research Description
Reteaching	When students have not demonstrated mastery of concepts/content, teachers should feel free to reteach the concepts/content without unproductive pressure to get through the curriculum guide by a deadline set by people who are disconnected from the classroom and the individual needs of the learner. Rather than an inch deep and a mile wide, instruction should be a mile deep and an inch wide. Superficial knowledge of myriad concepts is not an antecedent for student achievement and school improvement.
Standards for Writing in Every Lesson	Many students detest writing because it has frustrated them, but often it is not their fault; they simply have not been taught the writing process. Each lesson in the Integrated Approach should have a writing component through which students must respond to a content-related writing prompt that requires them to justify their response with information stated in or inferred from the text.
Year-Round Accommodations	Be careful to ensure that students with IEPs and 504s are receiving the accommodations as outlined in official documents. Students are likely to reject accommodations made by staffers who magically appear on state assessment days to act as scribes, readers, and the like. For example, if a student's IEP states that he or she should have a reader for testing opportunities, that requirement applies to every test during the school year.

Table 2.3—Quadrant II: Instructional Imperatives
(continued)

Integrated Approach Component	Action-Research Description
Meaningful Work for English Language Learners	English language learners can learn the skills to be assessed at their own individual pace. Will they be able to make inferences that require a cognitive leap without an ability to read academic English? They probably cannot, but math is a universal language, and foundational skills for reading/English as identified by your state curriculum can easily be taught to your English language learners. Keeping them busy with coloring or ignoring them instructionally because they do not present problem behaviors is not fair to them. Give them academic work, and you will be amazed with how many skills they will master in a short period of time. My ELL population led my school in gains after one year, achieving gains in excess of 50% in both reading and mathematics, just because we taught them.
Use Manipulatives to Teach Abstract Mathematical Concepts	Students who struggle in mathematics need manipulatives to learn abstract concepts. A mathematics classroom without manipulatives is in danger of failing to promote enduring understanding of concepts. To shift the learning paradigm from number sense and basic computation to abstract concepts requires manipulatives as a bridge.
Bell to Bell Instruction	Why are kids across the nation instructed by adults to line up and wait for the bell to ring?

Table 2.3—Quadrant II: Instructional Imperatives
(continued)

Integrated Approach Component	Action-Research Description
Minimize Instructional Interruptions	Instructional leaders must protect precious instructional time by: Disallowing "all calls" during the school day with the exception of emergencies. Disallowing or limiting room to room calls during class time. Disallowing calls from administrators and guidance counselors into classrooms. (Can't the administrators and counselors walk to the room to retrieve the student(s) they need without interrupting instruction for 20 or more other learners?) Disallowing secretaries to call into classrooms to give lunch money, homework assignments, or PE uniforms to kids who left these items at home (all these calls can be made at the change of class or students can be located by the secretary during lunchtime).
Emergency-Only Hall Passes for First and Last 10 Minutes of Class	Arguably the most crucial instructional moments are at the beginning and end of a lesson. For this reason, in this approach, students must have an authentic emergency to receive a hall pass during the introduction of concepts/content and the independent assessment at the close of the lesson.

Table 2.4—Quadrant 3: Data Analysis

Integrated Approach Component	Description
Meetings with Below-Grade-Level Performers and Parents	Each student who reads or does mathematics below the state standard should meet with the principal and at least one parent or guardian to discuss the student's previous year's performance. The school should identify strengths and weaknesses, set academic goals, and provide parents and students with tools they can use together at home to close the achievement gap (e.g., a reading workbook with skills linked to the state curriculum or a multiplication table for students who lack automaticity).
Coded Seating Charts with Previous Performance	Many educators talk about knowing the learner, but how many really know their students' performance level on the previous year's mandated, state assessments? With this approach, each classroom should have a coded seating chart that gives the teacher and the qualified observer information about mathematics and reading levels, special education, and ELL status. For example: The names of students who did not pass the state assessment would have their name underlined once; those who met standards would have their name underlined twice; those who exceeded standards would have their name underlined three times. Students who are receiving special education services would have their name with a period next to it, while students who speak English as a new language would have an asterisk following their name. These codes cannot be shared with the students; they are for the use of the adults in the building and are to be used only to meet the needs of divergent learners.

Table 2.4—Quadrant 3: Data Analysis
(continued)

Integrated Approach Component	Description
Pre-Tests and Post-Tests	The standards/objectives/assessment limits that will be tested in select grades at the elementary, middle, and high school level should be taught and assessed throughout the school year. Students' only exposure to the assessment limits cannot be your system's essential curriculum. Students should receive daily instruction and short-cycle assessments to ascertain levels of skill attainment for the purpose of reteaching to the threshold of mastery. (See Chapter 5.)
Progress Charts in Each Classroom (Data Centers)	For maximum impact, use student identification numbers to post student progress on the weekly pre-test/post-test. Students who are aware of their progress on the standards/objectives/assessment limits that will be assessed are likely to hold attitudes and engage in behaviors that support skill attainment. For some students, their experience with success on the weekly pre-test/post-test may be their first experience with academic success. Once they experience success, they will want the experience over and over again as it is contagious. (See Chapter 6.)
Monthly Reporting of Pre-Test/Post-Test Data	Once a month, after teaching and assessing four skills, the grade-level team leader (for elementary schools) or the content-area leader/department chair (middle and high schools) should report the gains made by students in the grade-level meeting or in the departmental meeting for all to celebrate.

Table 2.4—Quadrant 3: Data Analysis
(continued)

Integrated Approach Component	Description
Progress Reports Every Two and a Half Weeks	Although your school system may require a progress report only every five weeks, in this approach to instructional leadership, parents receive a progress report every two and a half weeks. Parents love it!
Needs-Specific Seminar Courses	Students who have an identified deficit in reading/English and/or mathematics are registered for a 10-week seminar taught by a highly skilled teacher immediately following homeroom. Students who are proficient or better on the previous year's administration of the state exam are exempt from such a class and are allowed to select an interest-based seminar on the subject of their choice or participate in band or choir during this time.
Item Analyses	By content area, teachers review student responses on locally written quarterly assessments in reading/English, mathematics, science, and social studies to identify trends in student responses. The team of teachers uses data from commonly missed questions to make instructional decisions for reteaching and future planning.

Table 2.5—Quadrant 4: Administrative Support

Integrated Approach Component	Description
Professional Development Series	In order to build faculty and staff knowledge of each of the four components of the Integrated Approach, it will be necessary to develop a year-long professional development calendar facilitated by site-based instructional leaders, teacher leaders, and central office personnel. Since time for PD is limited, make use of: • Faculty meeting time to run concurrent sessions that repeat throughout the first semester to ensure that all faculty and staff have an opportunity to attend. • "In-school" administrative planning time. • Full-day, systemwide professional development days. • Content meetings. • After-school time (you may have to seek funding to support this initiative). (See Appendix A for sample PD topics.)
Timely Informal Feedback	Each qualified observer should be responsible for informally observing five teachers per week and providing written feedback aligned with the components and considerations found in your school's newly formed/revised Culture of Instruction. (See Appendix B for Integrated Approach: Informal Observation Checklist.)

Table 2.5 — Quadrant 4: Administrative Support
(continued)

Integrated Approach Component	Description
Co-Planning and Co-Teaching with Qualified Observer	This approach requires teachers to submit to an instructional paradigm shift. In order to assist teachers in this transition, it will be useful to teachers to co-plan performance-based objectives and explicit instruction with the support of a qualified observer. Participating teachers should have increased support to plan and facilitate changes in their instructional practices with confidence and fidelity to the approach.
No Late Homework Policy	There are probably many schools of thought on accepting late homework, but this approach is as much about teacher/administrator accountability as it is about student accountability. To that end, this schoolwide approach to increasing rigor and achievement works well when students are not allowed to submit late homework. All late homework should receive a zero. It teaches students to be responsible for their work, and it sends a strong message to the home. One might think that this policy is too harsh, but even with this policy in place, nearly 65% of my current school's population earned honor roll status in quarter 1, 2, 3, and 4 in all grades. Students learned that homework was non-negotiable.

Table 2.5 — Quadrant 4: Administrative Support
(continued)

Integrated Approach Component	Description
Grading for Accuracy	Homework should be graded for accuracy, rather than for "effort," the all-popular and subjective method for grading. Without grading for accuracy, how does the teacher get information to drive instructional decisions following a lesson or a series of lessons? It may also be useful to decide upon the weight (in percentage points) for classwork, homework, and tests/quizzes—and to be consistent across grade levels and content areas.
Homework Bank	A number of students may need additional practice on the standards/objectives/ assessment limits that will be tested on your state-mandated assessment outside of the school day. For that reason, it would be useful to collect and organize a set of homework assignments and keys on each assessment limit across ability levels and content areas. For example, a middle school might have a sixth-, seventh-, and eighth-grade social studies-related assignment to find the main idea.
Saturday Academy for Special Needs and English Language Learners	Repetition and practice are keys to for the development of skill attainment for students with special needs and English language learners. It will be useful to invite these student groups to school on weekends for small group instruction in groups not to exceed five, taught by an expert in reading for one hour and mathematics for another hour. After two years of implementation, 71% of my current school's special needs population are proficient or better in reading; that's up from 21% in 2006, prior to the implementation of the Integrated Approach. Similar gains were made in mathematics.

Table 2.5—Quadrant 4: Administrative Support
(continued)

Integrated Approach Component	Description
Special Education Self-Contained Teachers as Content Experts	Most teachers are in this profession because they have a love for children and teaching. Even with those good intentions, it is difficult to become an expert on three or more subjects. Requiring special education teachers to teach multiple subjects contributes to underperformance among students with special needs. Students with special needs deserve to be exposed to your system's Essential Curriculum by a teacher who has mastery-level knowledge of the content. In this approach, self-contained classroom special educators teach one subject across grade levels, which allows them the opportunity to attend content meetings and countywide content-area professional development.
Special Education Inclusion Teachers as Content Experts	You also want your inclusion teachers to become experts in the content areas, so spreading them too thin can also work against your school improvement efforts. Placing your inclusion teacher in English and mathematics courses is useful because reading and math IEP goals can be met under special education laws, and skills taught in these two subjects transcend the other content areas.

Table 2.5—Quadrant 4: Administrative Support
(continued)

Integrated Approach Component	Description
Paraprofessionals as Providers of Support in Social Studies and Reading Courses	Assigning your instructional assistants/ paraprofessionals to meet the needs of your special education population in social studies and reading allows you to build the individual capacity of staffers in a limited number of content areas. Keep in mind that reading teachers are the most skilled people in your building in teaching reading skills; they do not necessarily need a full-time co-teacher; a well-trained instructional assistant is sufficient. Special education law does not dictate that students receive reading support in reading classes only. We used this approach, and now more than 90% of my current school's population reads at proficiency level or better—after having failed to demonstrate adequate yearly progress for the previous two consecutive years.

Table 2.5 — Quadrant 4: Administrative Support
(continued)

Integrated Approach Component	Description
Teacher Planning Time: *Monday* Grade-Level Team Meetings *Tuesday* Parent/Teacher Conferences *Wednesday* Teacher Choice *Thursday* Student Support Meetings *Friday* Assessment Limit Planning	Your system's master agreement has parameters for the use of daily planning time. Know the parameters and make effective and efficient use of the time each week to support approach implementation. Be sure to use one day for teachers to meet to discuss how they plan to introduce the upcoming week's standards/objectives/assessment limit for the week as a grade-level team (elementary schools) or content area (middle and high schools).
Consistent Consequences for Disruptive Students	Once you have implemented this approach, one of the bonus outcomes will be a significant reduction in disruptive student behavior. After all, students will be less frustrated with learning and therefore less likely to act out for the purpose of avoiding academic work. However, with a new, schoolwide focus on rigor and individual student needs, it will be important to have an agreed-upon set of clearly communicated consequences for behavior that disrupts teaching and learning, as well as appropriate follow-through. Teachers will thank you for it.

CHAPTER THREE

Establishing the Imperative—
Examine the Data

> *"Schools are data wealthy, so go beyond*
> *using data to inform and use data to help*
> *teachers and students to perform."*

As determined by student performance on the 2003 administration of your state's standardized assessment, all public, state-funded schools are expected to demonstrate a measure of incremental academic growth until the 2013–14 school year, when all student groups are to reach 100% proficiency in reading and mathematics. In order to demonstrate adequate yearly progress (AYP), each student group must meet the prescribed annual measurable outcome (AMO), which again is determined by how well, or how poorly, students in your state performed on the aforementioned 2003 benchmark assessment in your state. For example, Maryland's AMOs for elementary reading and mathematics are as follows:

Table 3.1—Elementary AMOs (Reading and Mathematics)
2003–2014 by Percentage

Year	Reading	Math
2003	43.8	41.1
2004	46.3	44.1
2005	57.8	53.6
2006	62.5	58.8
2007	67.2	63.9
2008	71.8	69.1
2009	76.5	74.2
2010	81.2	79.4
2011	85.9	84.5
2012	90.6	89.7
2013	95.3	94.8
2014	100.0	100.0

NOTE: From Maryland State Department of Education website

As you can see from Table 3.1, the average annual increase for gains required to demonstrate AYP is 4.7% for reading and 5.2% for mathematics. In other words, not only would your students who scored as proficient or better in the previous year need to continue to read at the state standard, but an additional 4.7% of the tested population (grades 3, 4, and 5 in this case) would need to reach proficiency in reading. Likewise, an additional 5.2% of the tested population also must reach proficiency in mathematics for an elementary school in Maryland to achieve adequate yearly progress each successive year (there are exceptions to this rule that will discussed later in this chapter).

Consider this. If instruction were to remain unchanged in your school/system, are all student groups likely to meet the moving AMO? This question cannot be answered with confidence without the following two-step analysis of student performance data. Instructional leaders, in conjunction with the site-based leadership team, must conduct this data analysis. In doing so, the imperative for implementing this approach will be strengthened.

ANALYZING THE DATA

Step 1: Identify the previous year's reading/English and mathematics AMOs for your state (it differs slightly for elementary, middle, and high schools across the states).

This information is readily available on your state's website.

Step 2: Use the Integrated Approach Projection Template to report the performance of the aggregate for the previous school year and make a projection for the upcoming two years for reading/English and mathematics.

To complete step 2:
- Identify the number of students who took the reading/English assessment; be aware that ELL (English language learners) students are exempt from the reading/English test their first year in the country—row 1.
- Identify the number of students who took the mathematics assessment (ELL students are not exempt from the mathematics test their first year in the country because math is seen as a universal language)—row 1.

- Identify the number of students who actually scored as proficient or better on the math and reading assessments for the previous year—row 2.
- Calculate the total number of students in your aggregate above or below the AMO for the previous year—row 3.
- Use the AMO for the upcoming two years in reading/English and mathematics to make a projection of the number of students needed to demonstrate AYP for the two consecutive years to come—rows 4 and 5.

Table 3.2—Integrated Approach Sample Projection
Ruth E. Tolden Lane Elementary School

Reading/English 438 and Mathematics 440 Students
Tested in Grades 6–8
2008–09 Reading/English AMO 76.5% and Mathematics 74.2%

	Tested Area Reading	Tested Area Math
# of Students Needed to Demonstrate AYP, 08–09	335.07	326.48
# of Students Who Actually Demonstrated AYP, 08–09	351	261
# of Students Over or Under AMO Threshold, 08–09	+15.93	-65.48
# of Students Under or Above 09–10 AMO	-4.66	-88.36
# of Students Under or Above 10–11 AMO	-25.24	-110.80

NOTE: *Doing the calculations should give you and your team an idea of how your students will perform if instruction remains the same for the upcoming school years.*

Without major changes in instructional approach or demographics, this school isn't likely to be able to demonstrate AYP for the upcoming school years in both mathematics and reading. If you think this analysis spells trouble, remember that this chart merely represents the aggregate. If the aggregate is struggling to pass the state-mandated assessment, imagine the performance status of the disaggregated groups. Complete step 3 in the data analysis framework to further set the imperative for the implementation of the Integrated Approach.

Step 3: Use the Student Group Analysis Template to report the previous year's performance of each of the five possible race-based student groups and three possible service-based student groups. Your state sets the number of students necessary to form a student group. For example, Maryland uses September 30th enrollment of five students from any race/ethnicity and service group to form a reported group. Know your state's requirements; they may differ from Maryland. The most effective time for this data sharing is on the first preservice day prior to the beginning of the school year; it will serve as a catalyst to focus everyone on the common cause (student achievement)—or take this step at least one month prior to implementation.

- See Table 3.3 to complete step 3 in this approach and do the following for both mathematics and reading ...
- Identify the percentage of proficient or better students from each race-based and service-based group in your school (column 2).
- Determine the number proficient in each student group and set up a ratio (column 3).

- Calculate the number by which each student group met or missed the AMO; multiply that year's AMO for reading or math by the total number of test takers in the group and subtract that number from the number proficient in that student group (column 4).

If a student group missed the AMO, calculate the number of students by which each student group met or missed the confidence interval to get a clearer picture of the performance of that group. (The confidence interval is one of the exceptions to the rule determining how schools can make AYP.) If a student group missed the AMO, then your state may consider your student group a passing group if they scored within a +/- range. The larger the student group, the smaller the confidence interval range. Conversely, the smaller the student group, the larger the confidence interval range. This allowance represents test writers' sensitivity to students who may have had a bad testing day. To calculate the number of students in your school that met or missed the confidence interval, multiply the number of test takers in reading/English by the low-band percentage of the confidence interval. That tells you how many students you needed to demonstrate AYP to meet the interval. Then subtract that number from the number of students who were actually proficient; then do the same for mathematics (column 5).

Table 3.3—Sample Integrated Approach Student
Group Analysis
S. Hamlin, Jr. Middle School
Mathematics Proficiency 2006–07
660 Test Takers

Student Group	Percentage Proficient	Number Proficient	Met/Missed AMO by ___ Students	Met/Missed Confidence Interval by ___ Students
All Students	62.5%	430:660	Met by 100	
African American	57.4%	165:287	Met by 21.5	
Native American/ Native Alaskan	NA	NA	NA	
Asian	84.1%	53:63	Met by 21.5	
Hispanic	56.6%	43:76	Met by 5	
White	71.9%	166:231	Met by 50	
Free/Reduced Meals	48.3%	73:151	Met by 2.5	
Special Education	9.4%	5:53	Missed by 21.5	Missed by 11.5
English Language Learners	22.7%	5:22	Missed by 11	Met by .45
2006–07 Mathematics AMO -50%				

NOTE: *Complete this analysis for both reading/English and mathematics. This step will invariably convince your faculty and staff of the imperative to change "the way things have always been done."*

CHAPTER FOUR

Analyzing the Demands
of the State Curriculum

> *"The nuanced demands of the state
> curriculum should be reflected
> in daily instruction."*

In accordance with federally mandated legislation (enacted in 2002), each state department of education has composed and published a statewide curriculum for reading/English and mathematics. Parenthetically, some states have even developed state curricula for social studies, sciences, and the applied academics (art, music, world languages, and physical education). The focus of this approach is the transferability to reading/English skills across the content areas and the natural link of mathematics skills to science instruction.

Each state has identified standards for reading and correlated learning objectives linked to each standard, as well as assessment limits derived from the larger objectives. In your state's reading/English curriculum, you will invariably find two important standards: (1) Comprehension of Informational Text and (2) Comprehension of Literary Text. Every state expects students to be able to read informational and literary text, demonstrate comprehension of what they read, and make higher order connections to the text. Your state's test writers use the assessment limits (which are linked to the larger learning objective) to create your state's annual, standardized assessment. Even if your state does not use the term "assessment limit," it is useful for readers across the nation to use a common term to communicate these core skills. Assessment limits in your state curriculum are the skills that will be assessed on your state's standardized assessment and represent the "least that should be taught in the classroom" and the "most that will be assessed by the state."

Let me be clear. No one, including this writer, is advocating teaching only the assessment limits and ignoring your system's essential curriculum, but I urge you to make certain that students have a firm foundation in the assessment limits. The assessment limits are the prerequisites to reading and doing math on or above grade level. Allow me to trace for you the development of an assessment limit in the Maryland State Curriculum (MSC).

Standard:	Comprehension of Informational Text
Indicator:	Developing and applying comprehension skills by reading a variety of self-selected and assigned print and electronic informational texts
Objective:	Identify and use text features to facilitate an understanding of informational texts
Assessment Limit:	Use print features such as: large bold print, font size/type, italics, colored print, quotation marks, underlining, and other print features encountered in text

Adapted from Maryland State Curriculum.

Yes, these skills are embedded in your school system's essential curriculum, but for many students who have traditionally underperformed on standardized assessments this assessment limit is buried in the curriculum. Below-average and average readers do not actively use print features to understand what they read and cannot evaluate how the inclusion of such print features impact their ability as readers to grasp the underlying meaning that the author intended, which is a demand placed on eighth-graders nationally on standardized assessments. Teaching this skill in a reading unit for a day or two will not necessarily translate into students reaching mastery-level understanding of the assessment limit. In order to promote high levels of student achievement, assessment limits must become explicit in daily instruction across grade levels and content areas.

The following is an illustration why an average student has difficulty passing a state assessment written below grade level and why an above-average student does not always score as advanced. (Did you know that state assessments are written below grade level?) In many school systems, there are cognitive gaps in the essential curriculum. For example, at random, ask one of your students (middle or high school student) to give you the meaning of the Latin base word greg-. (While you're at it, ask a teacher or two and see what answer you get. You'll be amazed with the responses you receive.) Ask a student the meaning of this base word because it's commonly used on state assessments and the SAT/GRE, and students will likely encounter words derived from greg- in informational or literary texts.

If a student knows the meaning of the Latin base word greg-, and common base words like it, they might have a fighting chance of answering the litany of close-ended vocabulary questions, analogies, and vocabulary-in-context questions commonly found on standardized assessments. The Latin base word greg- means group and gives students a key to unlocking the meaning words like:

> **egregious** (prefix e- meaning out; suffix –ous meaning full of)—egregious, meaning fully standing out from the group

congregate, segregate, aggregate, gregarious, disaggregate—and the list goes on.

But where in your system's essential curriculum is this skill taught? In which content area(s) in your school are word parts actively and consistently taught to students as a skill necessary for navigating text containing unfamiliar words and fully understanding what they read? Word parts (base words and affixes) appear in your state curriculum, so it's certain that students will be asked questions on standardized assessments to test their knowledge of them. Thus a failure to teach them explicitly is neglectful and harmful to student achievement. Asking students to use a word in a sentence does not result in enduring knowledge of the word's definition. However, a student who understands word parts can determine the meaning of just about any multi-syllabic, unfamiliar word.

In fact, research suggests that a student who reads below grade level has an operational vocabulary bank of only 2,500 words, but needs one that consists of 25,000 words in order to function at grade level or above. Exposing students to this assessment limit (word parts) quickly multiplies their vocabulary tenfold and, for a significant number of students, pushes them from Basic to Proficient, Proficient to Advanced, or Advanced to a perfect score. You do know that gifted students should be scoring near-perfect scores on a state assessment written below grade level? Right?

It has been my experience in implementing this approach and coaching others in the implementation process that two-thirds of the students who score Basic, below the state standard, on their reading/English assessment, miss the pass rate by only one or two questions, so imagine the impact of exposing students to assessment limits: print features and word parts. If you stopped with these two assessment limits, the landscape of your students' scores would change overnight. This approach does much more: It guarantees that all of your students, regardless of race/ethnicity and service group status are systematically exposed to a significant number of your state's assessment limits by teachers who understand the demands of the assessment limits and speak a common language of instruction across grade levels and content areas.

For tangible examples, on the next several pages, you will find the Maryland (elementary, middle, and high school) assessment limits for informational and literary texts. Upon analysis, you will find that the primary-grade-level assessment limits have striking similarities with the secondary assessment limits. Note that the high school assessment limits have a significant emphasis on grammar and are not separated into informational and literary text assessment limits. You also will find equally interesting nuances in how the assessment limits are tested, which shows the need for changes in delivering instruction as your faculty and staff develop an in-depth understanding of the demands of the assessment limits.

NOTE: My current school in Maryland focused on student and teacher understanding of the following select middle school informational and literary text assessment limits—and easily brought our school out of School Improvement Status in record time.

One of the elementary schools in Las Vegas that implemented this approach had not demonstrated AYP in five consecutive years, but after five months of implementation, made AYP by exceeding 22% gains in reading/English and mathematics for all student groups, with significantly larger gains for previously underperforming student groups.

Table 4.1
High-Impact State Curriculum
Assessment Limits for Informational Text (2.0)

ELEMENTARY GRADES—25

Assessment Limits
Prefixes
Base words
Suffixes
Vocabulary-in-context
Text/print features (and contribution to meaning)
Graphic aids
Informational aids
Organizational aids
Main idea
Identifying supporting details (evaluating importance of details)
Fact and opinion
Making inferences
Drawing conclusions

Adapted, along with other charts on pages 49–75, from Maryland State Curriculum; please check your own state's curriculum website.

Table 4.1
High-Impact State Curriculum
Assessment Limits for Informational Text (2.0)

ELEMENTARY GRADES—25
(continued)

Assessment Limits
Making generalizations
Organizational patterns and associated phrases: • Sequential and chronological order • Cause and effect • Problem/solution • Similarities and differences • Description • Main idea and supporting details
Summarizing
Paraphrasing
Author's opinion
Author's purpose/text purpose
Comparing and contrasting
Identifying similes, metaphors, and personification
Idioms
Tone
Connotation and denotation
Determining the impact of repetition

Table 4.2
High-Impact State Curriculum
Assessment Limits for Literary Text (3.0)

ELEMENTARY GRADES—28

Assessment Limits
Prefixes *
Base words *
Suffixes *
Vocabulary-in-context *

Table 4.2
High-Impact State Curriculum
Assessment Limits for Literary Text (3.0)

ELEMENTARY GRADES—28
(continued)

Assessment Limits
Text/print features * (and contribution to meaning)
Graphic aids ^* (and contribution to meaning)
Informational aids ^* (and contribution to meaning)
Organizational aids ^* (and contribution to meaning)
Main idea *
Distinguishing among narrative texts
Elements of a story (grade 5—problem, exposition, rising action, climax, and resolution)
Identifying details that create setting and mood
Analyzing characters (traits, motivations, and personal growth and development)
Explaining relationships between/among characters, setting, and events
Drawing conclusions about the narrator (based on thoughts and observations)
Explaining the meaning of words, lines, and stanzas in poetry
Explaining sound elements of poetry (rhyme, rhyme scheme, alliteration, and onomatopoeia)
Tone *
Explaining stage directions
Universal theme
Paraphrasing *
Summarizing *
Explaining personal connections to the text
Connotation and denotation (grade 5) *

Table 4.2
High-Impact State Curriculum
Assessment Limits for Literary Text (3.0)

ELEMENTARY GRADES—28
(continued)

Assessment Limits
Figurative language * Simile, metaphor, and personification
Repetition and its contribution to meaning
Explaining the believability of characters' actions and events
Making predictions and asking questions (if the text were extended)

NOTE:
^ = *Different aids and features than those found in informational text*
* = *Skill overlap from informational text*

Table 4.3
High-Impact State Curriculum
Assessment Limits for Informational Text (2.0)

MIDDLE GRADES—31

Assessment Limits
Prefixes
Base words
Suffixes
Vocabulary-in-context
Text/print features (and contribution to meaning)
Graphic aids (and contribution to meaning)
Informational aids (and contribution to meaning)
Organizational aids (and contribution to meaning)
Main idea

Table 4.3
High-Impact State Curriculum
Assessment Limits for Informational Text (2.0)

MIDDLE GRADES—31
(continued)

Assessment Limits
Identifying supporting details (evaluating importance of details)
Fact and opinion
Making inferences
Drawing conclusions
Making generalizations
Organizational patterns (sequential and chronological order, cause and effect, problem/solution, similarities and differences, description, and main idea and supporting details)
Author's purpose/text purpose
Author's argument
Author's viewpoint
Explaining how organizational patterns support text purpose
Summarizing
Paraphrasing
Comparing and contrasting
Identifying similes, metaphors, and personification
Bias
Idioms
Author's tone
Analyzing effect of repetition on meaning
Evaluating fulfillment of reading purpose
Connotation and denotation
Analyzing the reliability of information
Identifying persuasive techniques

Table 4.4
High-Impact State Curriculum Assessment Limits
for Literary Text (3.0)

MIDDLE GRADES—34

Assessment Limits
Text features ^*
Graphic aids ^*
Organizational aids ^*
Informational aids ^*
Analyzing plot events (exposition, rising action, climax, and resolution)
Distinguishing narrative texts (short stories, folklore, realistic fiction, science fiction, historical fiction, fantasy, essays, biographies, autobiographies, personal narratives, and plays)
Identifying details that create setting and mood
Identifying connections between/among characters, setting, and mood
Analyzing characters (traits, motivations, and personal growth and development)
Analyzing relationships between/among characters, setting, and events
Analyzing internal/external conflicts that motivate characters/advance plot
Flashback
Foreshadowing
Conclusions about the narrator (based on his or her thoughts and observations)
Analyzing the meaning of words, lines, and stanzas (in poetry)
Figurative language (in poetry) simile, metaphor, personification
Analyzing sound elements of poetry (rhyme, rhyme scheme, alliteration, and onomatopoeia)

Table 4.4
High-Impact State Curriculum Assessment Limits
for Literary Text (3.0)

MIDDLE GRADES—34
(continued)

Assessment Limits
Tone * (including tone of a character)
Mood
Analyzing effect of stage directions
Analyzing action of scenes and acts and impact on meaning
Main idea *
Universal theme
Paraphrasing *
Summarizing *
Idioms and colloquialisms *
Denotation and connotation *
Imagery and its contribution to meaning
Hyperbole and exaggeration
Rhetorical questions
Plausibility of plot and credibility of characters
Asking questions and making predictions (if the text were extended)
Author's/text purpose *
Explaining personal connections to the text

NOTE:

^ = *Different aids and features than those found in informational text*

* = *Skill overlap from informational text*

Table 4.5
High-Impact State Curriculum Assessment
Limits for English

HIGH SCHOOL—61

Assessment Limits
Prefixes
Root words
Suffixes
Text features (sidebars, time lines, charts, subheadings, diagrams, illustrations, and photographs)
Identifying text purpose/author's purpose
Words with multiple meanings
Colloquialisms
Idioms
Connotation and denotation
Paraphrasing
Summarizing
Analyzing plot elements (exposition, rising action, climax, turning point, and resolution)
Foreshadowing
Flashback
Analyzing cause and effect
Analyzing characters (traits, motivations, and personal growth and development)
Identifying details that create setting and mood
Analyzing internal/external conflicts that motivate characters/advance plot
Analyzing author's perspective
Analyzing point of view
Determining theme (key terms, issues, ideas, and emotions—two or more texts)
Main idea/central ideas

Table 4.5
High-Impact State Curriculum Assessment
Limits for English

HIGH SCHOOL—61
(continued)

Assessment Limits
Determining the influence, effect, or impact of historical, cultural, or biographical information on a text
Identifying organizational patterns and evaluating their effectiveness (sequential and chronological order, cause and effect, problem/solution, similarities and differences, description, and main idea and supporting details)
Determining tone (author's and characters')
Analyzing effect of repetition
Hyperbole and exaggeration
Figurative language (simile, metaphor, personification, alliteration, assonance, and onomatopoeia)
Allusion
Analogy
Imagery
Symbolism
Evaluating the effectiveness of stylistic elements
Comparing and contrasting styles of writing (formal, informal, conversational, scholarly, journalistic, and poetic)
Distinguishing among types of irony (verbal, situational, and dramatic)
Drawing conclusions
Evaluating sources of information (for accuracy, honesty, and reliability)
Author's credentials, url extension (.gov versus .alt), and webmaster contact information
Citing references

Table 4.5
High-Impact State Curriculum Assessment
Limits for English

HIGH SCHOOL—61
(continued)

Assessment Limits
Grammar assessment limits
Parallelism
Identifying and using coordinating conjunctions
Identifying and using subordinate/dependent clauses
Using topic sentences and supporting details
Identifying sentence fragments
Identifying run-on sentences
Identifying and using compound sentences
Using transition words between sentences and paragraphs
Understanding and correcting modifiers (placement, misplaced, and dangling)
Identifying prepositional phrases
Identifying restrictive and non-restrictive clauses
Correcting shifts in person, number, and verb tense
Spelling of commonly confused words
Identifying and correcting errors for end punctuation
Identifying and correcting errors for five rules of comma usage (in a series, after introductory statements, setting off appositives and parenthetical statements, in dates and places, and before coordinating conjunctions in compound sentences)
Identifying and correcting errors for rules of semi-colon usage (between closely related main clauses)
Identifying and correcting errors for rules of apostrophe usage
Identifying and correcting capitalization for proper nouns, proper adjectives, geographic places, businesses, organizations, and institutions

Table 4.5
High-Impact State Curriculum Assessment
Limits for English

HIGH SCHOOL—61
(continued)

Assessment Limits
Distinguishing and using passive versus active voice
Subject and verb agreement
Pronoun and antecedent agreement
Classifying words and phrases

The same is true of mathematics instruction across the nation. Students are promoted from one grade to the next without having mastered the assessment limits from the previous grade. This phenomenon is evidenced by student performance on your system's quarterly mathematics assessment at the close of each quarter and by student performance on your state's standardized assessments year after year. If students are failing the intermittent quarterly assessments, which are composed of the same type of questions as your state assessment, it is almost guaranteed that they will perform at the same level on the state assessment. To score differently requires a systematic intervention to ensure that students are taught to mastery on each assessment limit by teachers who understand the demands of the assessment limit and can both teach and assess students' performance.

Classrooms across the nation are populated with students who failed to master the prerequisite skills for math instruction at their grade level. For example, a third-grader who has not mastered the use of skip counting to extend and work backwards or complete number patterns with missing numbers in grade

3 will likely be one who has difficulty conceptualizing the rules for increasing and repeating patterns in grade 4. He or she may become a student who has difficulty applying the two-operation rule to extend number patterns in grade 5 and later become a student who has severe difficulty with a one-operation rule function table in grade 6. This student may ultimately become one who struggles with two-operation function tables in grade 7 and analyzing tables and algebraic functions in grade 8 and beyond.

NOTE: Conduct the same analysis of the mathematics assessment limits that you did for reading/English. Notice how mastery of the previous year's assessment limits is correlated with the potential of mastery for the next year.

Table 4.6
High-Impact State Curriculum Assessment Limits—Grade 3

OBJECTIVE	ASSESSMENT LIMITS (28)
STANDARD 1	**Knowledge of Algebra, Patterns, and Functions**
Patterns	Use skip counting to extend and work backward; include non-numeric patterns.
Expressions	Write numeric expressions.
Number Sentences	Find the missing number.
Number Lines	Graph whole numbers and proper fractions.
STANDARD 2	**Knowledge of Geometry**
Polygons	Identify triangles, quadrilaterals, pentagons, hexagons, or octagons and the number of sides or vertices.
Quadrilaterals	Identify squares, rectangles, rhombi, parallelograms, trapezoids, and the length of sides.

Table 4.6
High-Impact State Curriculum Assessment Limits—Grade 3
(continued)

OBJECTIVE	ASSESSMENT LIMITS (28)
Composite Figures	Identify triangles, rectangles, or squares as parts.
Cubes	Identify the number of edges, faces, vertices, or shape of each face.
Congruent Figures	Identify congruent figures.
Transformations	Use horizontal slide, flip over a vertical line, or turn 90 degrees clockwise around a given point of a geometric figure or picture.
Symmetry	Analyze figures and pictures.
STANDARD 3	Knowledge of Measurement
Measurement Units and Tools	Read and measure in customary and metric units; include length, time, temperature, and weight.
Perimeter and Area	Place on a grid.
Equivalent Measurements	Identify units of length.
STANDARD 4	Knowledge of Statistics
Tables	Organize and display data; interpret tables.
Pictographs	Organize and display data; interpret pictographs.
Bar Graphs	Single bar graphs; organize and display data; interpret bar graphs.
STANDARD 5	Knowledge of Probability
Probability	Describe in words; use probability terms of more (or most) likely, less (or least) likely, or equally likely.
STANDARD 6	Knowledge of Number Relationships and Computation/Arithmetic
Expanded Form	Express whole numbers in expanded form.
Place Value	Identify place value in whole numbers 0–9,999.

Table 4.6
High-Impact State Curriculum Assessment Limits—Grade 3
(continued)

OBJECTIVE	ASSESSMENT LIMITS (28)
Comparing/ Ordering Whole Numbers	Identify whole numbers 0–10,000.
Fractions	Represent fractions as parts of a region or set; use denominators of 2, 3, or 4.
Currency	Represent money amounts in different ways; determine the value of a set of mixed currency.
Odd and Even Numbers	Identify whole numbers.
Addition	Use whole numbers with no more than three addends, with no more than three digits.
Subtraction	Use whole numbers with no more than three digits.
Multiplication and Division	Represent basic facts of no more than $9 \times 9 = 81$.
Properties	Identify and use the commutative, identity, or zero properties.

Table 4.7
High-Impact State Curriculum Assessment Limits—Grade 4

OBJECTIVE	ASSESSMENT LIMITS (26)
STANDARD 1	Knowledge of Algebra, Patterns, and Functions
Function Tables	Complete using a one-operation rule.
Patterns	Extend use of skip counting; generate rules for growing and repeating patterns.
Expressions	Write numeric expressions; determine equivalent expressions.
Equations	Solve using multiplication.
Number Lines	Graph proper fractions and mixed numbers.

Table 4.7
High-Impact State Curriculum Assessment Limits—Grade 4
(continued)

OBJECTIVE	ASSESSMENT LIMITS (26)
Coordinate Plane	Identify ordered pairs in the first quadrant.
STANDARD 2	**Knowledge of Geometry**
Angle Relationships	Identify acute, right, or obtuse angles.
Solid Geometric Figures	Identify cones, cylinders, prisms, and pyramids; describe pyramids and prisms by number of edges, faces, or vertices.
Transformations	Analyze translations, reflections, and rotations.
STANDARD 3	**Knowledge of Measurement**
Measurement Units and Tools	Read and measure in customary and metric units; determine equivalent units.
Perimeter and Area	Use polygons with no more than six sides (perimeter); rectangles (area).
Time	Determine start time, elapsed time, and end time.
STANDARD 4	**Knowledge of Statistics**
Line Plots and Line Graphs	Organize and display data; interpret line plots and line graphs.
Data Sets	Determine median, mode, and range.
STANDARD 5	**Knowledge of Probability**
Probability	Express as a fraction.
STANDARD 6	**Knowledge of Number Relationships and Computation/Arithmetic**
Expanded Form	Express whole numbers and decimals in expanded form.
Place Value	Identify place value in whole numbers 0–1,000,000.
Comparing/ Ordering Whole Numbers	Use whole numbers 0–1,000,000.
Comparing/ Ordering Fractions	Use fractions and mixed numbers with like denominators.

Table 4.7
High-Impact State Curriculum Assessment Limits—Grade 4
(continued)

OBJECTIVE	ASSESSMENT LIMITS (26)
Comparing/ Ordering Decimals	Use decimals 0–100 with no more than two decimal places.
Currency	Compare the value of sets of mixed currency.
Factors and Multiples	Use divisibility rules.
Whole Number Operations	Add, subtract, multiply, and divide whole numbers.
Fraction Operations	Add and subtract proper fractions and mixed numbers.
Decimal Operations	Add and subtract two decimals.
Estimation	Approximate the sum, difference, product, or quotient of two numbers.

Table 4.8
High-Impact State Curriculum Assessment Limits—Grade 5

OBJECTIVE	ASSESSMENT LIMITS (34)
STANDARD 1	Knowledge of Algebra, Patterns, and Functions
Function Tables	Write a rule for a one-operation table; complete a one-operation table.
Patterns	Apply a two-operation rule to extend.
Expressions	Write one-operation algebraic expressions; evaluate one-operation algebraic expressions.
Equations	Solve one-step equations.
Number Lines	Graph decimals and mixed numbers.
Coordinate Plane	Graph ordered pairs in the first quadrant.

Table 4.8
High-Impact State Curriculum Assessment Limits—Grade 5
(continued)

OBJECTIVE	ASSESSMENT LIMITS (34)
STANDARD 2	**Knowledge of Geometry and Measurement**
Line Relationships	Identify parallel or perpendicular lines and line segments.
Composite Figures	Identify polygons (triangles or quadrilaterals) within a composite figure.
Quadrilaterals	Classify and compare using sides and angles.
Solid Geometric Figures	Identify and classify pyramids and prisms.
Similar Figures	Identify and describe.
Transformations	Analyze translations, reflections, and rotations.
STANDARD 3	**Knowledge of Measurement**
Measurement Units	Estimate and determine weight, mass, and capacity.
Measurement Tools	Measure length to 1/8 inch; measure an angle between 0 and 180 to the nearest degree.
Perimeter and Area	Use polygons with no more than eight sides (perimeter); rectangles (area); given closed figures on a grid.
Time	Determine start time, elapsed time, and end time.
Equivalent Units	Use seconds, minutes, and hours or pints, quarts, and gallons.
STANDARD 4	**Knowledge of Statistics**
Stem-and-Leaf Plots	Organize and display data; interpret stem-and-leaf plots.
Line Plots and Line Graphs	Organize and display data; interpret line plots and double line graphs.

Table 4.8
High-Impact State Curriculum Assessment Limits—Grade 5
(continued)

OBJECTIVE	ASSESSMENT LIMITS (34)
Double Bar Graphs	Organize and display data; interpret double bar graphs.
Circle Graphs	Interpret circle graphs.
Data Sets	Determine mean.
STANDARD 5	**Knowledge of Probability**
Outcomes	Determine possible outcomes of two independent events.
Probability	Express as a fraction; make predictions.
STANDARD 6	**Knowledge of Number Relationships and Computation/Arithmetic**
Equivalent Fractions	Identify and determine equivalent forms of proper fractions.
Comparing/ Ordering Fractions	Use fractions and mixed numbers.
Comparing/ Ordering Decimals	Use decimals 0–100 with no more than three decimal places.
Prime and Composite Numbers	Identify whole numbers 0–100 as prime or composite.
Factors	Use divisibility rules; identify the greatest common factor (GCF).
Multiples	Identify common multiples and the least common multiple (LCM).
Whole Number Operations	Multiply and divide whole numbers.
Fraction Operations	Add and subtract proper fractions and mixed numbers with answers in simplest form.
Decimal Operations	Add and subtract decimals, including money; multiply by a whole number.
Estimation	Approximate the sum, difference, and product of decimals; approximate the product and quotient of whole numbers.

Table 4.9
High-Impact State Curriculum Assessment Limits—Grade 6

OBJECTIVE	ASSESSMENT LIMITS (29)
STANDARD 1	**Knowledge of Algebra, Patterns, and Functions**
Function Tables	Write a rule for a one-operation table; complete a table with a two-operation rule.
Expressions	Write one-operation algebraic expressions; evaluate one-operation algebraic expressions.
Order of Operations	Evaluate numeric expressions.
Writing Equations and Inequalities	Use a variable, relational symbol, and operational symbol to represent relationships.
Equations	Solve one-step equations.
Number Lines	Graph integers (-20 to 20).
STANDARD 2	**Knowledge of Geometry and Measurement**
Coordinate Plane	Graph ordered pairs of integers and fractions/mixed numbers.
Line Segments	Identify diagonals of a polygon.
Parts of a Circle	Find radius, diameter, or circumference.
Triangles	Classify using sides and angles; find the missing angle; measure and find the area.
Angle Relationships	Identify perpendicular bisectors or angle bisectors.
STANDARD 3	**Knowledge of Measurement**
Measurement Tools	Measure length to 1/16 inch.
Volume	Use rectangular prisms.
Composite Figures	Find the area; use no more than four polygons (triangles or rectangles).
Perimeter and Area	Find the missing dimension of a quadrilateral, given perimeter or area.

Table 4.9
High-Impact State Curriculum Assessment Limits—Grade 6
(continued)

OBJECTIVE	ASSESSMENT LIMITS (29)
STANDARD 4	**Knowledge of Statistics**
Frequency Tables	Organize and display data; interpret frequency tables.
Stem-and-Leaf Plots	Organize and display data; interpret stem-and-leaf plots.
Circle Graphs	Analyze circle graphs.
STANDARD 5	**Knowledge of Probability**
Simple Probability	Express as a decimal.
Experimental Probability	Make predictions and express as a fraction, decimal, or percentage.
STANDARD 6	**Knowledge of Number Relationships and Computation/Arithmetic**
Exponential Form	Represent whole numbers (0–100,000).
Equivalent Rational Numbers	Determine equivalent forms of fractions as decimals, percentages, or ratios.
Comparing/ Ordering Rational Numbers	Use fractions and decimals, alone or mixed together.
Whole Number Operations	Add, subtract, multiply, and divide (grades 3–5).
Fraction Operations	Add, subtract, and multiply fractions and mixed numbers with answers in simplest form.
Decimal Operations	Multiply decimals; divide decimals by a whole number.
Percentage	Determine percentage of a whole number; use 10%, 20%, 25%, or 50%.
Properties	Use the distributive property to simplify expressions.
Estimation	Approximate the product or quotient of two decimals.

Table 4.10
High-Impact State Curriculum Assessment Limits—Grade 7

OBJECTIVE	ASSESSMENT LIMITS (37)
STANDARD 1	Knowledge of Algebra, Patterns, and Functions
Function Tables	Complete a table with a two-operation rule.
Writing Expressions	Write one- and two-operation algebraic expressions.
Evaluating Expressions	Evaluate one- and two-operation algebraic expressions, including fractions and decimals.
Order of Operations	Evaluate numeric expressions, including decimals.
Writing Equations and Inequalities	Use a variable, relational symbol, and up to two operational symbols to represent relationships, including fractions and decimals.
Equations	Solve one- and two-step equations, including fractions and decimals.
Inequalities	Solve one-step inequalities; graph solutions on a number line.
Formulas	Apply given formulas to a problem-solving situation.
Number Lines	Graph rational numbers (-100 to 100).
Coordinate Plane	Graph ordered pairs of rational numbers (-20 to 20).
Tables	Identify change of values as increase, decrease, or have no change.
STANDARD 2	Knowledge of Geometry and Measurement
Angle Relationships and Measures	Use vertical, adjacent, complementary, or supplementary angles.
Quadrilaterals	Find the missing angle measure.
Congruent Polygons	Determine congruent parts.

Table 4.10
High-Impact State Curriculum Assessment Limits—Grade 7
(continued)

OBJECTIVE	ASSESSMENT LIMITS (37)
Transformations	Perform translations, reflections, or rotations on the coordinate plane.
STANDARD 3	**Knowledge of Measurement**
Area	Use parallelograms and trapezoids.
Surface Area	Use rectangular prisms.
Scales	Use a given scale to determine missing measures.
STANDARD 4	**Knowledge of Statistics**
Stem-and-Leaf Plots	Organize and display data in back-to-back stem-and-leaf plots.
Data Displays	Recognize faulty interpretation or representation of data; determine the best choice of display.
Measures of Central Tendency	Determine and apply mean, median, and mode.
STANDARD 5	**Knowledge of Probability**
Sample Space	Determine number of outcomes.
Independent Probability	Express probability of two independent events as a fraction, decimal, or percentage.
Experimental Probability	Make predictions and express as a fraction, decimal, or percentage.
STANDARD 6	**Knowledge of Number Relationships and Computation/Arithmetic**
Exponential Notation	Express in standard form.
Expanded Form	Express decimals in expanded form.
Equivalent Rational Numbers	Determine equivalent forms of fractions, decimals, percentages, or ratios.
Comparing/ Ordering Rational Numbers	Use fractions, decimals, or integers.
Whole Number Operations	Add, subtract, multiply, and divide (grades 3–5).

Table 4.10
High-Impact State Curriculum Assessment Limits—Grade 7
(continued)

OBJECTIVE	ASSESSMENT LIMITS (37)
Integer Operations	Add, subtract, multiply, and divide integers (-100 to 100).
Fraction Operations	Add, subtract, and multiply positive fractions and mixed numbers.
Decimal Operations	Add, subtract, multiply, and divide (grades 4–6).
Powers and Square Roots	Calculate powers of integers using exponents of no more than 3; calculate square roots of perfect square whole numbers.
Laws of Exponents	Simplify expressions using power times power or power divided by power.
Properties	Use the commutative, associative, or identity properties to simplify expressions.
Estimation	Approximate the sum, difference, product, or quotient of rational numbers.
Rates and Ratios	Determine equivalent ratios; use rates, unit rates, and percentages as ratios.

Table 4.11
High-Impact State Curriculum Assessment Limits—Grade 8

OBJECTIVE	ASSESSMENT LIMITS (38)
STANDARD 1	Knowledge of Algebra, Patterns, and Functions
Sequences	Extend arithmetic and geometric sequences.
Linear Relationships	Determine if a relationship is linear or non-linear from a graph.
Writing Expressions	Write algebraic expressions with up to three operations.
Evaluating Expressions	Evaluate algebraic expressions with up to three operations and rational numbers.

Table 4.11
High-Impact State Curriculum Assessment Limits—Grade 8
(continued)

OBJECTIVE	ASSESSMENT LIMITS (38)
Order of Operations	Evaluate numeric expressions, including rational numbers (-100 to 100) and absolute value.
Writing Equations and Inequalities	Use a variable, relational symbol, and up to three operational symbols to represent relationships.
Equations	Solve multi-step equations, including rational numbers.
Inequalities	Solve one- and two-step inequalities; graph solutions on a number line.
Equivalent Equations	Identify equivalent multi-step equations.
Formulas	Apply given formulas to a problem-solving situation.
Linear Equations	Graph on a coordinate plane.
Slope	Determine slope from a graph.
STANDARD 2	Knowledge of Geometry and Measurement
Angle Relationships and Measures	Alternate interior, alternate exterior, or corresponding angles.
Pythagorean Theorem	Find the missing sides of right triangles; apply to real-world problems.
Similar Polygons	Determine similar parts; find missing measures.
Transformations	Multiple transformations including translations, reflections, or rotations on the coordinate plane.
STANDARD 3	Knowledge of Measurement
Circles	Find circumference and area.
Composite Figures	Find total area using triangles, rectangles, or circles.
Volume	Use cylinders.

Table 4.11
High-Impact State Curriculum Assessment Limits—Grade 8
(continued)

OBJECTIVE	ASSESSMENT LIMITS (38)
Proportional Reasoning	Use proportions to solve measurement problems, including scale drawings.
STANDARD 4	**Knowledge of Statistics**
Tables	Interpret tables; analyze data.
Circle Graphs	Organize and display data; interpret circle graphs.
Box-and-Whisker Plots	Organize and display data; interpret box-and-whisker plots.
Scatter Plots	Organize and display data; interpret scatter plots.
Data Displays	Recognize faulty interpretation or representation of data; determine the best choice of display.
STANDARD 5	**Knowledge of Probability**
Sample Space	Determine number of outcomes.
Probability	Use independent and dependent probability; express as a fraction, decimal, or percentage.
Predictions	Analyze results of a survey/simulation; express probability as a fraction, decimal, or percentage.
STANDARD 6	**Knowledge of Number Relationships and Computation/Arithmetic**
Scientific Notation	Represent whole numbers (-10,000 to 1,000,000,000).
Equivalent Rational Numbers	Determine equivalent forms of fractions, decimals, percentages, or ratios (grades 4–6).
Comparing/ Ordering Rational Numbers	Use integers or positive rational numbers; include absolute value.
Fraction Operations	Add, subtract, and multiply positive fractions and mixed numbers (grades 4–7).

Table 4.11
High-Impact State Curriculum Assessment Limits—Grade 8
(continued)

OBJECTIVE	ASSESSMENT LIMITS (38)
Decimal Operations	Add, subtract, multiply, and divide (grades 4–6).
Integer Operations	Add, subtract, multiply, and divide integers (-1,000 to 1,000).
Powers and Square Roots	Calculate powers of integers using exponents of no more than 3; calculate square roots of perfect square whole numbers; estimate square roots.
Laws of Exponents	Simplify expressions using power times power or power divided by power.
Properties	Use the distributive, commutative, associative, inverse, or identity properties to simplify expressions.
Rates and Ratios	Determine unit rates; determine and use percentages, rates of increase/decrease, discount, commission, sales tax, and simple interest.

Table 4.12
High-Impact State Curriculum Focus Assessment Limits—
Algebra I/Data Analysis

OBJECTIVE	ASSESSMENT LIMITS (26)
	Algebra
Patterns	Extend patterns and functional relationships that are expressed numerically, algebraically, and/or geometrically; include tables.
Functions	Determine if a relation is a function; use numeric or graphic representations.
Integer Operations	Add, subtract, multiply, and divide (grades 7–8).

Table 4.12
High-Impact State Curriculum Focus Assessment Limits—
Algebra I/Data Analysis
(continued)

OBJECTIVE	ASSESSMENT LIMITS (26)
Fraction Operations	Add, subtract, multiply, and divide; include fractions and mixed numbers (grades 6–7).
Order of Operations	Evaluate numeric expressions (grades 6–8).
Writing Expressions	Write algebraic expressions (grades 6–8); describe a real-world situation (grade 8).
Laws of Exponents	Use laws of exponents to simplify expressions (grades 7–8).
Polynomial Expressions	Add, subtract, multiply, or divide to simplify polynomial expressions.
Writing Equations	Represent relationships; describe real-world problems (grades 6–8).
Solving Linear Equations	Solve a one-variable equation for the unknown.
Solving Linear Inequalities	Solve a one-variable inequality for the unknown.
Slope	Identify given linear relationships in a graph, table, or equation (grades 6–8).
Graphing Linear Equations	Graph a given equation, two or more collinear points, or a point and slope; include vertical lines.
Graphing Linear Inequalities	In a real-world context, include compound inequalities.
Systems of Equations	Solve systems of linear equations by graphing; include parallel lines; write systems.
Non-Linear Functions	Identify maxima/minima, zeros, rate of change (increasing/decreasing), domain and range, or continuity.
Formulas	Apply formulas to solve real-world problems.
Matrices	Represent data in tables; perform matrix addition, subtraction, or scalar multiplication.

Table 4.12
High-Impact State Curriculum Focus Assessment Limits—
Algebra I/Data Analysis
(continued)

OBJECTIVE	ASSESSMENT LIMITS (26)
	Data Analysis
Data Analysis	Analyze frequency tables, box-and-whisker plots, and other displays.
Measures of Central Tendency	Use mean, median, and mode to solve problems.
Measures of Variability	Use range, interquartile range, and quartiles to solve problems.
Experimental Probability	Calculate based on a given set of data.
Theoretical Probability	Calculate given a situation involving chance.
Making Predictions	Determine given data from a simulation or research.
Scatter Plots	Organize and display data; analyze scatter plots (grade 8).
Lines of Best Fit	Determine based on a given set of data.

CHAPTER FIVE

Develop an Action Plan for the Tested Areas

"The only change that occurs of its own volition is chaos."

After identifying the statewide assessment limits and the nuances of each assessment limit across grade levels, select the assessment limits to teach. Most states have an average of 30–50 assessment limits for each tested area (reading/English and mathematics). Once you have identified the assessment limits, construct an Action Plan Calendar and assign each assessment limit to a week of the school year for each tested area to be taught and assessed by teachers. By teaching the assessment limits explicitly, you are directly exposing your student body to the state assessment, one skill at a time. If your state curriculum has more assessment limits than weeks in the school year, prior to the state assessment the instructional leadership team, led by the principal, will need to decide which assessment limits will be taught and assessed.

Regardless of whether it's an elementary, middle, or high school, the following features of the Integrated Approach Action Plan are universal and should be implemented faithfully for optimal gains.

Table 5.1—Universal Integrated Approach:
Action Plan Features

Five to seven minutes of instruction on the assessment limit of the week is the drill prior to the beginning of EVERY lesson (there are some exceptions at the elementary school level that will be explained later in this chapter).
The five-question, multiple-choice pre-test on the skill must be administered on the first day of the week prior to instruction on the skill, and the same five-question post-test must be administered on the final day of the week to assess student acquisition of the skill. If you have short weeks in the calendar, you may wish to teach a skill that week without assessing it—or combine a short week with a five-day week to make an eight-day week to teach and assess a more challenging skill. Use your state's released item as a guide for composing tests.
The pre-test is the post-test (same questions). You may change the order of the questions if you think students will attempt to memorize the order of the questions.
Teachers should refrain from reviewing the questions on the pre-test; doing so will invalidate the post-test results at the end of the week.
Use your state curriculum glossary of terms to phrase the questions on the pre-test/post-test so students become accustomed to the terminology.
Use a teacher timer to ensure that teachers refrain from using excessive instructional time on the assessment limit drill; 5–7 minutes is sufficient.

Use a short-form Scantron for students to record their responses to the pre-test/post-test; it is easy to grade. The size of your staff will dictate the number of Scantron machines you will need to buy/lease, and the size of your student body will dictate the number of Scantrons you will need to purchase. Please don't allow a student to grade another student's pre-test/post-test; it will invalidate the data. You must be able to trust the data.

Record the post-test grade in the grade book. Students should be held accountable for their score on the post-test; after all, they will have had instruction on that assessment limit in multiple classes.

If students are absent for the pre-test, do not require them to take it upon their return. Just mark an "A" for absent in the spreadsheet that we will discuss later.

If students are absent for the post-test, they must take it upon their return; you will need their score for the spreadsheet and grade book.

Students will have demonstrated mastery of the assessment limit pre-test if given a score of 4 or 5. All students who scored a 0–3 should be required to take the post-test on the last day of the week.

Students who scored a 4 on the pre-test should be allowed to take the post-test in order to attempt to earn a 5.5.

The Related Arts teachers (music, art, physical education, etc.) teachers should teach only the first 10 informational text assessment limits. This allows them to contribute to the school improvement process after having been formerly left out. It is good for students to see that all subjects are related to the assessment limit skills.

The instructional leadership team should provide the faculty with materials to introduce each assessment limit to students—i.e., for "Prefix" week, each teacher should be given a list of prefixes and should be instructed to teach the prefixes that most closely relate to their content area. For "Making Inferences" week, each teacher should be provided with the graphic organizer to be used by all to teach the assessment limit.

Your action plan will differ depending upon the grade level of your school: elementary, middle, or high school.

Elementary schools should do the following for optimal results:

- Implement the plan in grades 3–5 only.
- Limit Related Arts teachers to teaching/assessing the first 10 informational text assessment limits only.

Because grade levels typically have different schedules and because elementary teachers are generalists (they teach all of the core subjects), decide which times of the day would lend themselves to the 5–7 minutes of assessment limit instruction. The school in Las Vegas referenced earlier in the text decided to teach the assessment limits on the following schedule:

- In Homeroom (Reading/English Assessment Limit of the Week).
- Before Lunch (Reading/English Assessment Limit of the Week).
- After Lunch (Mathematics Assessment Limit of the Week).
- In Related Arts (Reading Assessment Limit of the Week).
- Last Subject of Day (Mathematics Assessment Limit of the Week).

Even though reading skills are taught three times in this example, students would be tested only once on the Reading/English Assessment Limit of the Week. Your team should decide which part of the day is best for your students.

NOTE: If your students struggle more with mathematics than reading, then your team may decide to facilitate three opportunities for mathematics assessment limits and two for reading/English.

Middle schools should adhere to the following for optimal gains:

1. Compose a five-question, multiple-choice pre-test/post-test for each subject taught for each grade level: grades 6–8.

2. The reading assessment limits should be taught and assessed in reading, social studies, and Related Arts classes. (So on the first day of the week students will have four informational text assessment limit pre-tests and four on the last day of the week.) These tests should assess student knowledge of the assessment limit using a text related to the content area that assesses the skill (i.e., the social studies pre-test/post-test should use social studies related texts and so forth).

3. Related Arts teachers should teach and assess only the first 10 assessment limits.

4. The literary assessment limits should be taught and assessed in the English courses using literary text (if your school has a reading/English block, combine the informational and literary text assessment limits into one action plan).

5. The mathematics assessment limits should be taught and assessed in mathematics and science classes (the skill of the week for mathematics should be the same skill taught and assessed in science classes; if sixth-grade math is teaching and assessing ordered pairs, so is sixth-grade science).

High schools should follow the following procedures for optimal results:

1. Compose a five-question pre-test/post-test for each subject taught for each grade level that you will involve in the approach (typically grades 9–11, depending on the year students are required to take the state assessments).
2. The reading assessment limits for informational text should be taught in reading courses, social studies classes, and elective courses. (So on the first and last day of the week students may have several different informational text assessment limit pre-tests.) These tests should assess student knowledge of the assessment limit using a text related to the content area that assesses the skill. The Related Arts pre-test/post-test should use a text the teacher might use to teach Related Arts.
3. The literary assessment limits should be taught and assessed in English classes. If your school has no reading courses, the informational text and literary text assessment limits will need to be taught and assessed in English courses in the early high school grades.
4. The mathematics assessment limits should be taught and assessed in mathematics and science classes. (The skill of the week for mathematics should be the same skill taught and assessed in science classes; if ninth-grade math is teaching and assessing two-step algebraic equations, so is ninth-grade science.)

Regardless of your school's grade level, your instructional leadership team should facilitate professional development sessions on the how to teach each assessment limit. This professional development should take place prior to requiring the faculty and staff to teach and assess student knowledge of the assessment limits (see the discussion in Chapter 2 on the use of planning time—quadrant 4). Teachers must be taught the difference in cognitive demands for each assessment limit. In many cases, the instructional leaders will be learning along with the teachers and instructional assistants. This approach is not about PRIDE; rather it is about RESULTS. Your professional development must demystify the demands of the assessment limits to ensure that students acquire mastery-level knowledge and skill. For example, in Maryland a sixth-grader has to identify organizational aids, but an eighth-grader has to not only identify the organizational aid, but also evaluate the author's use of text features and explain how the inclusion of a particular aid contributes to meaning. In Arkansas, sixth- and seventh-graders have to identify alliteration in a literary text, but eighth-graders have to identify and differentiate between alliteration and assonance.

NOTE: On the next page you will find a sample Action Plan Calendar. There are just 24 weeks before the state assessment in this state (Maryland), so the plan for informational text assessment limits must reflect the system's calendar. In weeks with fewer than five school days, it is recommended that you teach the assessment limit each day, but skip testing it then.

> *"You must abort ego, tradition, comfort, and the ordinary in order to produce extraordinary results."*

SAMPLE ACTION PLAN CALENDAR FOR:
Assessment Limits for Informational Text

MIDDLE SCHOOL — 25

Assessment limits	Week of
Prefixes and base words	September 7
Suffixes	September 14
Vocabulary-in-context	September 21
Text/print features (and contribution to meaning)	September 28
Graphic aids (and contribution to meaning)	October 5
Informational aids (and contribution to meaning)	October 12
Organizational aids (and contribution to meaning)	October 19
Main idea and summarizing	October 26
Identifying supporting details (evaluating importance of details)	November 2
Fact and opinion	November 9
Making inferences	November 16
Drawing conclusions (teach only skill-short week, no pre-test/post-test)	November 23
Making generalizations	November 30
Organizational patterns (sequential and chronological order, cause and effect, problem-solution, similarities and differences, description, and main idea and supporting details)	December 7
Author's purpose/text purpose	December 14
Author's argument and author's tone (teach only skill-short week, no pre-test/post-test)	December 21
Author's viewpoint and bias	January 4
Explaining how organization supports text purpose	January 11
Paraphrasing (teach only skill-short week, no pre-test/post-test)	January 18
Comparing and contrasting	January 25
Idioms	February 1
Evaluating fulfillment of reading purpose (teach only skill-short week, no pre-test/post-test)	February 8

Assessment limits	Week of
Connotation and denotation	February 15
Analyzing the reliability of information	February 22
Identifying persuasive techniques	March 1

NOTE: Follow the same process for mathematics.

CHAPTER SIX

Reporting the Progress

"Momentum is indiscriminate."

When I developed the Integrated Approach in 2003, I had no idea that this step in the process would have such a profound impact on students, staff, and the bottom line. Students who have been unsuccessful academically have a heightened awareness of their shortcomings; they have anxiety about being in the classroom setting and have fears about being singled out as a low performer. In ways unimaginable, this step in the approach addresses and rectifies this impediment to student achievement and school improvement.

In this approach each classroom should have a highly visible data center that allows students to track their performance on the pre-tests and post-tests each week in order to promote awareness of individual and class performance. Students should to be taught how to use their individual performance to set academic goals for upcoming pre-tests and post-tests. They should be told that the weekly assessments really are the state exam, one skill at a time. Moreover, students should be aware of the correlation between their performance on the pre-test and post-test and their subsequent performance on the actual assessment. To that end, each week, students should be strongly encouraged to visit the data center in each of their classes.

One of the initially unintended, but promising, outcomes of this approach is the response that students have to being able to track their performance. They revel in their successes on the assessments, particularly those who had not previously experienced academic success. In many cases, learners who were formerly unmotivated and detached from instruction, race to the data center in each classroom to check their scores and celebrate their performance.

Below is an example of an Integrated Approach Data Center Spreadsheet and an explanation of each component.

Table 6.1—Integrated Approach Data Center Spreadsheet

Integrated Approach Informational Text Assessment Limits (Mohorn-Grade 6)	2008 MSA Designation	2008 MSA Score	Prefixes		Suffixes		Root Words		Vocabulary-in-Context		Text Features		Main Idea		ID Supporting Details		Fact and Opinion		Making Inferences	
Student ID#			Pre-Test	Post-Test	Pre-Test	Post-Test	Pre-Test	Post-Test	Pre-Test	Post-Test	Pre-Test	Post-Test	Pre-Test	Post-Test	Pre-Test	Post-Test	Pre-Test	Post-Test	Pre-Test	Post-Test
1 54484664	B	383	4	5	3	5	5													
2 62662616	A	435	3	4	2	4	4													
3 51515155	P	418	3	4	4	4														
4 51515151	B	383	2	3	4	4														
5 65151511	A	428	5	5	2	4														
6 26544155	P	403	4	4	0	3														
7 51515151	B	311	3	3	4	4														
8 51515151	A	424	5	5	3	4														
9 89416511	A	429	5	5	5	5														
10 51615154	P	414	2	4	3	4														
11 65626556	P	423	2	4	4	4														
12 51651511	P	424	5	5	2	4														
13 51519561	P	426	3	4	5	5														
14 65946516	B	310	4	4	1	4														
15 62654864	P	404	3	3	3	4														
16 96251516	P	409	3	2	5	5														
17 51616515	A	441	4	5	4	4														
18 61213156	A	458	3	4	2	4														
19 51654651	A	520	3	4	4	5														
20 65165150	B	335	2	4	5	5														
21 32600216	A	464	4	4	3	4														
22 00656546	A	541	5	5	5	5														
Number of Mastered			10	18	11	21	2	0	0	0	0	0	0	0	0	0	0	0	0	0
Number of Non-Mastered			12	4	11	1	0	0	0	0	0	0	0	0	0	0	0	0	0	0
Percentage Mastered			45%	82%	50%	95%	100%													

NOTE: *It may be useful to us this spreadsheet at parent/teacher conferences to apprise parents of their child's progress.*

The spreadsheet contains the following:

- A confidential student identification number (you should not use student names).
- Performance level (on the previous year's state assessment—below, at, or above state standard).
- Scale score (on previous year's state assessment).
- Pre-test score column for each assessment limit to be taught.
- Post-test score column for each assessment limit.

- Formulas at the bottom of the spreadsheet that calculate:
  - Number of students who scored 80% or better on the pre-test.
  - Number of students who did not score 80% or better on the post-test.
  - Percentage of students who mastered the pre-test and post-test.

This spreadsheet will differ depending on your school's grade level (elementary, middle, or high).

Elementary Schools

Since elementary teachers teach every core subject to the same students each day (for the most part) teachers in grades 3–5 will need one spreadsheet for the reading assessment limits and one spreadsheet for the mathematics assessment limits to be covered. Remember, even though it's recommended that you teach the assessment limits two or three times a day, you will compose only one pre-test/post-test for each assessment limit in your grade level.

Related Arts teachers will just need one spreadsheet for the first 10 assessment limits for each class that they teach. Remember that all Related Arts teachers will administer their own pre-test/ post-test related to their content for each of the 10 assessment limits that they will cover (one test for grade 3, one for grade 4, and one for grade 5 that reflects the increase in difficulty level of the assessment limit from grade 3 to grade 5). The informational text/literary text assessment limit spreadsheet should have students' level of performance and scale score from the previous year's reading/English state assessment.

The mathematics assessment limit spreadsheet should have students' level of performance and scale score from the previous years' mathematics state assessment.

Middle and High Schools

Since most middle school teachers teach one subject to the same students each day, teachers in grades 6–8 will need one spreadsheet for the each class populated with the assessment limits to be covered.

Related Arts teachers will just need one spreadsheet for the first 10 assessment limits for each class that they teach. Remember, Related Arts teachers will administer their own pre-test/post-test related to their content for each of the 10 assessment limits that they will cover (one test for grade 6, one for grade 7, and one for grade 8 that reflects the increase in difficulty level of the assessment limit from grade 6 to grade 8).

For reading, social studies and Related Arts teachers, the informational text assessment limit spreadsheet should have students' level of performance and scale score from the previous year's reading/English state assessment.

For English teachers, the literary text assessment limits spreadsheet should have the students' level of performance and scale score from the previous year's reading/English state assessment.

The mathematics assessment limit spreadsheet should have students' level of performance and scale score from the previous year's mathematics state assessment.

NOTE: Teachers are urged to use pre-test/post-test data to assign homework and create vacation review packets in order to guide their parent/teacher conference conversations and reteaching decisions.

In addition to reporting data for students, student performance on the pre-tests/post-tests should be published for the faculty and staff. At each monthly faculty meeting, grade-level meeting, or content-area meeting, it is prudent to share the performance of students on the pre-tests/post-tests. Sharing the data in this incremental manner creates enormous momentum and buy-in for the approach, and it allows teachers to see the impact of explicitly exposing student to the assessment limits each week. You will need to merge the data from each of the spreadsheets for each grade 3, 4, and 5 (elementary schools). This is beneficial to the teachers in each grade because it reveals students' strengths and weaknesses on each assessment limit by grade. A similar practice is recommended for middle schools and high schools. It is recommended that assessment limit data be reported by each subject area, rather than by grade. This practice allows each content area, including Related Arts, to see the impact of their contribution on student acquisition of new skills.

Do this each month to keep the staff motivated. Remember, the assessment limits are the state assessment presented in small pieces, one each week of the school year. Teachers and school leaders can even use this information to project student performance on the state assessment. Gains on the pre-tests/post-tests will invariably translate into gains on the state assessment. Below are sample monthly data reporting charts described above.

Table 6.2—Integrated Approach Monthly Four-Skill Reporting
Chart (Elementary)
September Reading/English Assessment Limits—Grade 4

Grade 4	Proficient on Pre-Test	Proficient on Post-Test	Gain
Prefixes	39%	89%	50%
Suffixes	25%	81%	56%
Base Words	41%	92%	51%
Vocabulary-in-Context	36%	74%	38%

NOTE: *Teachers will be amazed with the level of gains that their students will make after just three days of instruction on the assessment limits. You may even wish to report such data to parents at monthly PTA meetings.*

Table 6.3—Integrated Approach Monthly Four-Skill Reporting
Chart (Middle and High)
November Literary Text Assessment Limits—English Department

Grade 4	Proficient on Pre-Test	Proficient on Post-Test	Gain
Author's Argument	24%	78%	54%
Author's Viewpoint	19%	65%	46%
Author's Perspective	20%	82%	62%
Bias	24%	54%	30%

NOTE: *The data indicate that most students are still struggling with bias and may need more support with this assessment limit through homework assignments, after-school help, or through conversations with parents who are able to work with them at home on the skill.*

Table 6.4—Integrated Approach Monthly Four-Skill Reporting
Chart (Elementary)
September Math Assessment Limits—Grade 3

Grade 3	Proficient on Pre-Test	Proficient on Post-Test	Gain
Multiplying Whole Numbers	54%	88%	34%
Dividing Whole Numbers	25%	65%	40%
Adding/ Subtracting Fractions	18%	45%	27%
Multiplying Fractions and Mixed Numbers	9%	42%	33%

NOTE: *The data indicate that grade 3 students made significant gains on adding/subtracting fractions and multiplying fractions and mixed numbers, but there is still a great deal of work to be done on those skills. The point of celebration, however, should not be diminished; there was a 27% and a 33% gain in student understanding of these assessment limits, respectively.*

Table 6.5—Integrated Approach Monthly Four-Skill Reporting
Chart (Middle and High)
February Mathematics Assessment Limits—Science Classes

	Proficient on Pre-Test	Proficient on Post-Test	Gain
One-Step Inequalities	44%	69%	25%
Two-Step Inequalities	35%	71%	36%
Applying a Given Formula	14%	56%	42%
Graphing on a Coordinate Plane	2%	24%	22%

NOTE: *The data indicate that most students are still struggling with applying a given formula and even more with graphing on a coordinate plane. The math and science teams will need to meet to discuss a plan of action for this skill.*

CHAPTER SEVEN

Composing Higher Order Objectives

> *"It is not the neighborhood that results in underachievement; rather it is the instruction in the neighborhood that matters."*

All over the United States, teachers are teaching content and students are learning the facts of the content areas, as they should. In science, students learn that matter exists in phases; in English, students learn iambic pentameter; and in social studies, students are taught to memorize parts of the U.S. Constitution and a few key amendments. But, all too often, to the detriment of student achievement a vital component is absent from daily instruction. That key component is cognitive pluralism.

I remember instruction from my own days in primary and secondary schooling in Texas. My social studies teacher introduced me to the U.S. Constitution. I memorized parts of the document and, to this day, can recall and restate facts about its structure as follows: The U.S. Constitution consists of a preamble, seven articles, signers, and amendments. But so what? What did I gain beyond an ability to retain facts? The teacher failed to teach me to do something with my knowledge of the components of the Constitution. All I was taught to do was regurgitate information (content) in the same manner in which it was disseminated—and ingested. I was not required to use my new knowledge to perform a meaningful and relevant task.

More than five decades ago, Benjamin Bloom headed a group of educational psychologists who developed a classification of levels of intellectual behavior salient to the process of teaching and learning. Bloom (1956) found that more than 95% of the questions students were asked required them only to think at the lowest possible level … information recall (sounds an awful lot like my primary and secondary experience). Bloom identified six levels within the cognitive domain, from the simplest level—recall or recognition of facts through increasingly more complex and abstract mental levels—to the highest level, which is now classified as creating. Although Bloom's research has been widely accepted as useful for the purpose of planning and facilitating instruction representative of cognitive pluralism, many schools have yet to find ways to integrate what they know about cognitive demands into daily instructional practices. This brief, but essential chapter, will delineate the action steps for composing daily objectives that promote higher levels of thinking and doing for all students, regardless of ability.

The following simple changes in the delivery of instruction on the U.S. Constitution would have taken my teacher's unit from mediocre activity to rigorous intellectual work by requiring students to do one or more of the following:

1. Use their knowledge of the structure of the U.S. Constitution to compare and contrast it to the Magna Carta.
2. Compare and contrast the function of the U.S. Constitution and the Magna Carta.

3. Trace and explain the influence of the Magna Carta on modern constitutional law in the English- speaking world.
4. Evaluate the effectiveness of the U.S. Constitution's structure and clarity of word choice.
5. Create a new and improved constitution for a fictitious society using the U.S. Constitution and Magna Carta as guides.

Assigning students to engage in these activities requires them to recall information, demonstrate a profound level of understanding of the content, apply newly acquired knowledge in a new way, analyze the parts of a whole, evaluate ideas and make judgments, and construct a new product or point of view in the creative process. All students—regardless of race/ethnicity, socioeconomic status, limited English proficiency or exceptionality—should be exposed to such instruction on a daily basis.

To that end, daily objectives should be performance-based and have the following characteristics:

Table 7.1—Characteristics of Performance-Based Objectives

#	Characteristic	Explanation of Characteristic
1	A Content-Related "KNOW"	The KNOW represents the prerequisite content-related knowledge or skill that students must have or know in order to be able to demonstrate mastery of the "in order to" statement in the objective.
2	A Higher Order "DO"	The DO represents that which students are expected to be able to do by the close of the lesson or a series of lessons. It is always measurable/quantifiable and is always linked to a state assessment limit or a higher order thinking skill.

NOTE: Mathematics objectives are performance-based objectives by nature and therefore are NOT required to fit this format, but all other subjects, including Related Arts objectives, should be written using this model.

Following are some sample objectives that do not meet the performance-based criteria with an accompanying critique, possible rewrite, and an explanation of the rewrite. All performance-based objectives begin with SWBAT (students will be able to).

Objective 1:

Students will be able to use a jigsaw to state the main idea in a portion of a text.

Critique:

Yes, students do need to know how to state the main idea of a portion of a text. That is a useful skill, but what does that skill have to do with using a jigsaw? If a teacher is going to use an activity like a jigsaw as a vehicle to teach a skill and assess student understanding of content/concepts, fine, but the word "jigsaw" has no place in an objective. A jigsaw represents an activity. Performance-based objectives must be composed of a KNOW related to the content, followed by an "in order to statement" that requires students to DO something with their knowledge/skill.

Possible rewrite:

Students will be able to identify the supporting detail in order to determine the main idea of a portion of a text.

Explanation of rewrite:

- The KNOW is identifying supporting detail and the DO is determining the main idea.
- The KNOW is content-related prerequisite knowledge of the DO.
- The DO is an assessment limit and represents higher order thinking.

Objective 2:

Students will be able to analyze the extent to which the author fulfills the writing purpose on page 62.

Critique:

The extent to which the author fulfills the writing purpose should be taught and assessed in reading and English classes, but this objective does not include the prerequisite knowledge or skill that should accompany the higher order task. Furthermore, the specific page number of the text to be used should not appear in the objective. It may impede student ability to view the author's purpose as a skill limited to page 62 of that text, rather than a universal skill that can be used to evaluate any text in any content area.

Rewrite:

Students will be able to identify print features in order to analyze the extent to which the author fulfills the writing purpose.

Explanation of rewrite:

- The KNOW is identifying print features and the DO is analyzing the extent to which the author fulfills the writing purpose.
- The KNOW is content-related prerequisite knowledge/ skill for the DO.
- The DO is an assessment limit and represents higher order thinking.

Objective 3:

Students will be able to describe the Stamp Act as a cause of the American Revolution.

Critique:

The objective is "content-driven" much like the objectives from my own primary and secondary schooling—and like the objectives in many classrooms across the nation. Undoubtedly, students should learn about the Stamp Act, and they should know that it was related to the American Revolution, but this objective will require students only to memorize facts and does not represent cognitive pluralism.

Possible rewrite:

Students will be able to describe the structure and function of the Stamp Act in order to formulate a bill for a legislative vote.

Explanation of rewrite:

- The KNOW is describing the structure and function of the Stamp Act, and the DO is formulating a bill for a legislative vote.
- The KNOW is content-related prerequisite knowledge of the DO.
- The DO is an assessment limit and represents higher order thinking.
- The word "function" in the rewrite promotes a discussion of the Stamp Act as a cause of the American Revolution.

Below are examples of objectives that meet the Performance-Based (Cognitively Plural) Criteria across grade levels and content areas:

1. Students will be able to (SWBAT) identify the parts of a cell in order to classify cells as plant or animal.
2. SWBAT identify the impact of Christianity on Ancient Rome in order to analyze the effects of religion on the larger society.
3. SWBAT identify the components of setting and plot in order to analyze details that contribute to meaning.
4. SWBAT identify the main idea of a text in order to compose an original paraphrase.
5. SWBAT distinguish between fact and opinion in order to make inferences.
6. SWBAT analyze informational text in order to determine the sequential order of events.
7. SWBAT identify the main idea and supporting details in order to determine the author's purpose.

8. SWBAT identify the characteristics of all living things in order to classify and categorize organisms.
9. SWBAT distinguish between potential and kinetic energy in order to explain the Law of Conservation of Energy.
10. SWBAT list and explain the main characteristics of a civilization in order to relate them to a hierarchy of human needs.
11. SWBAT identify the purposes for reading in order to make judgments about the effectiveness of words and phrases used to persuade a reader.
12. SWBAT analyze literary elements in order to interpret figurative language.
13. SWBAT analyze a passage of literary text in order to distinguish between dynamic and static characters.
14. SWBAT identify the process of genetic coding in order to compare inherited and acquired traits.
15. SWBAT analyze the leadership of selected European missionaries in order to compare them to leaders of modern society.
16. SWBAT analyze the Stamp Act in order to defend it as a major cause of the American Revolution.
17. SWBAT analyze the Magna Carta and the U.S. Constitution in order to compare and contrast documents central to the formulation of federal law.
18. SWBAT identify bias in order to evaluate the reliability of information.
19. SWBAT identify events of the plot in order to analyze connections between characters, setting, and plot.
20. SWBAT to analyze primary sources in order to determine the influence, effect, or impact of historical, cultural, or biographical information on a text.

CHAPTER SEVEN: COMPOSING HIGHER ORDER OBJECTIVES

21. SWBAT identify important events in order to make predictions.

22. SWBAT identify different types of text in order to predict the author's purpose.

23. SWBAT identify the components of a fairy tale in order to compare and contrast U.S. versions with European versions.

24. SWBAT identify the cause of an event in order to determine its effect.

25. SWBAT identify context clues in order to determine the meaning of unfamiliar words.

CHAPTER EIGHT

Planning Explicit Instruction

> *"Student achievement is the by-product
> of knowing how to teach what you teach."*

Masterfully written curricula do not guarantee student achievement and school improvement. Rather, I have found that the delivery of instruction in conjunction with a spiral curriculum bolsters academic performance. As I stated in Chapter 2, a learning community with a true culture of instruction has agreed to a common set of theories, standards, and practices, one of which includes a single lesson plan format to be used across grade levels and content areas. Without a singular lesson plan format that transcends content areas, it is difficult to evaluate instruction by the same standards schoolwide, and is unnecessarily complicated for teachers to co-plan and co-teach efficiently and effectively.

The Integrated Approach Explicit Lesson Plan Format is based on the Pearson and Gallagher (1993) gradual release of responsibility model in that it requires students to take on more responsibility for skills acquisition as the lesson progresses, ending with a formative assessment in the independent setting. After linking instruction to a reading/English or mathematics assessment limit, teachers should:

- Compose an objective that links the content to a higher order thinking skill.

- Plan a five- to seven-minute drill to expose students to an assessment limit.

- Connect the new learning to students' prior knowledge.

- Introduce new content/concepts and define unfamiliar vocabulary words found in the text to be used.

- Address common misconceptions that students might have concerning the content/concepts.

- Model the learning outcome while students listen for the purpose of being able to independently perform the same task at the close of the lesson.

- Allow students to lead the teacher, demonstrating a developing understanding of the learning outcome (be sure to focus on the students with the lowest ability because their responses are the litmus test for the readiness of the entire class to proceed to the next step in the lesson).

- Place students in cooperative learning groups to practice, while the teacher circulates, assessing student understanding and assisting where necessary (groups of 2 or 3 are optimal and should have students with divergent levels of ability, if possible, in order to promote peer coaching).

- When students have demonstrated readiness, require them to demonstrate individual mastery of the learning outcome without any assistance from the teacher or their peers.

- Revisit the objective and measure student performance by quantifying the number of students who successfully completed the independent assessment to the threshold of mastery.

- Assign homework related to the learning objective (only take this step if students completed the independent activity successfully).

- Reflect, reflect, reflect.

Below you will find the Integrated Approach Explicit Instruction Lesson Plan Format.

Integrated Approach
Explicit Instruction Lesson Plan Format

Daily Objective/Learning Outcome
(Must include a content-related KNOW and a higher order DO)
Students will be able to:

_____

_____

_____

Drill/Motivation:
(Always related to the Focus Assessment Limit of the week)

_____

_____

_____

Connecting Prior Knowledge or Real-World Connection to Content:

_____

_____

_____

Introducing New Learning/Subject Matter:
(Introduce new concepts/content and define unfamiliar vocabulary words.)

_____

_____

_____

Teacher Model/Think Aloud:
(Students listen without participating for the purpose of being able to perform the same task in cooperative and independent settings.)

_____

_____

_____

Teacher-Led/Student Think Aloud:
(Students think aloud, demonstrating their new understanding of the content/concept in the cooperative setting for all to hear.)

_____

_____

_____

Cooperative Practice:
(Students are placed in small groups to work together to perform a task that demonstrates their understanding of the content/concept while the teacher circulates, assessing and assisting.)

Independent Test:
(Students demonstrate an individual understanding of the content/concept through writing while the teacher provides no assistance; the classroom should be silent, and the teacher should circulate as students work to gather data.)

Closure:
(The teacher revisits objectives, quantifies student performance using data from the independent test to determine next steps.)

Homework:
(This is directly linked to the daily objective.)

Teacher Reflection:
(The teacher reflects on the scope and sequence of the lesson, student acquisition of content/concept, and pacing.)

NOTE: After planning a few lessons using this format, you will be relieved by how little time (5–10 minutes) it takes to plan a solid lesson. Keep in mind that not all lessons will follow this format (e.g., a science lab or an exploratory lesson), but most lessons can and should adhere to the format.

APPENDIX A

Integrated Approach:
Professional Development Seminars

SAMPLE

Composing Higher Order Objectives
Facilitator: Principal
Required for teachers new to school

Understanding the State Curriculum and Assessment Limits
Facilitator: Principal
Required for teachers new to school

Writing Explicit Lesson Plans (Reading, English, Social Studies, Science)
Facilitator: Qualified observer
New teachers encouraged to attend

Paraprofessionals, an Integral Part of Instruction
Facilitator: Special education team leader
All paraprofessionals required to attend

Student Achievement and English Language Learners
Facilitator: ELL teacher
All teachers required to attend

Writing Explicit Lesson Plans and Using Manipulations for Math Instruction
Facilitator: Math team leader
All math teachers required to attend

The Role of Walk-Through Observations
Facilitator: Assistant principal (qualified observer)
All teachers required to attend

High-Impact Reading Strategies for Low-Performing Readers
Facilitator: Reading specialist
All teachers required to attend

Planning and Co-Teaching (Focus on Accommodations)
Facilitator: Special education team leader
Co-teachers required to attend

Backward Mapping and Long-Term Planning
Facilitator: Qualified observer
All teachers required to attend

Promoting Achievement Through Authentic Intellectual Instruction
Facilitator: Qualified observer
All teachers required to attend

Accessing Homework Banks and Connecting to Your Curriculum
Facilitator: Assistant principal
All teachers required to attend

NOTE: All sessions/workshops should be facilitated in years 1 and 2 of implementation in lieu of faculty meetings and should run concurrently.

APPENDIX B

Integrated Approach:
Informal Observation Checklist

(With a focus on Authentic Intellectual Instruction)

Name: _____ Date: _____

Course: _____ Time: _____

What I observed today included:

_____ **Higher order thinking**
Instruction was characterized by students using or manipulating knowledge as in analysis, interpretation, synthesis, and evaluation, as opposed to reproducing knowledge in previously stated forms.

_____ **Depth of knowledge**
Instruction addressed the central idea(s) of a topic or discipline with enough thoroughness to explore connections and relationships and to produce demonstrated, complex understanding.

_____ **Substantive conversation**
Students engaged in extended conversational exchanges with the teacher and/or their peers about the subject matter in a way that built an improved understanding of ideas or topics.

_____ **Value beyond school**
Students made connections between substantive knowledge and either public problems or personal experiences outside of school. *

* The first four items of this checklist are adapted from Newmann et al., 2001.

_____ **Objective was linked to essential curriculum and state assessment limit**

_____ **Majority of students were actively engaged**

_____ **Teacher used formative assessment to check for understanding**
The teacher assessed student understanding of idea(s)/topic(s) throughout the lesson in varied ways.

_____ **General and special educator worked effectively as a team (if applicable)**
Effective use of co-teaching model or small group instruction and accommodations for students were measurable and appropriate for students with special needs.

Comments:

_____
_____
_____
_____
_____
_____

APPENDIX C

Integrated Approach to Student Achievement Implementation Rubric

Key Terms
- **FARMS** (free and reduced meals)
- **Essential Curriculum**—your school system's curriculum
- **Assessment Limit**—the most that will be assessed by the state on the CRT (criterion-referenced test) and the least that should be taught in the classroom
- **CRT**—otherwise known as your annual state test (tests student ability on mastery of assessment limits as outlined in your state curriculum)

Teacher Expectations
- All students in the teacher's class—including those receiving FARMS, Special education services, and ELL (English language learners) services—are succeeding on assessment limits. **(Reflects Exemplary Implementation of Model; 5 points)**
- All students in the teacher's class—including those receiving FARMS, Special education services, and ELL services—may not be succeeding on assessment limits, but the teacher is aware of the challenge and can explain the plan for addressing it. **(Reflects Consistency with Model; 4 points)**
- All students in the teacher's class—including those receiving FARMS, Special education services, and ELL services—are failing on assessment limits. Although the teacher is aware of the challenge, the teacher cannot articulate the plan for addressing it. **(Lacks Consistency with Model; 2 points)**
- All students in the teacher's class—including those receiving FARMS, Special education services, and ELL services—are failing on assessment limits, and the teacher is unaware of the challenge. **(Lacks Consistency with Model; 0 points)**

Culture of Instruction

- The teacher, as a member of the professional learning community, uses language, approaches, and methodologies for teaching the essential curriculum that mirror those used by other teachers at the school and those discussed in schoolwide/ departmental professional development. **(Reflects Exemplary Implementation of Model; 5 points)**
- The teacher uses language, approaches, and methodologies for teaching focus skills that resemble those used by other teachers at the school and those discussed in schoolwide/departmental professional development. **(Reflects Consistency with Model; 3 points)**
- The teacher does not discuss instruction with other teachers at the school and does not use common language, approaches, and methods for teaching. **(Lacks Consistency with Model; 0 points)**

Staff Awareness of the Imperative

- The staff member is fully aware of longitudinal performance data on the CRT (criterion-referenced test) and on other tests related to the assessment limits for individual students and for student groups at the school. **(Reflects Exemplary Implementation of Model; 5 points)**
- The staff member does not know how individual students performed on the CRT and on other tests related to the assessment limits over time. **(Lacks Consistency with Model; 3 points)**
- The staff member does not know how student groups at the school have performed on the CRT and on other tests related to the assessment limits over time. **(Lacks Consistency with Model; 0 points)**

Demands of the State Curriculum

- The teacher is thoroughly familiar with the components of the essential curriculum and how it aligns with the state curriculum for reading and/or mathematics. **(Reflects Exemplary Implementation of Model; 5 points)**
- The teacher has a developing understanding of the components of the essential curriculum and how it aligns with the state curriculum for reading and/or mathematics. **(Reflects Consistency with Model; 4 points)**
- The teacher is familiar only with the essential curriculum. **(Lacks Consistency with Model; 2 points)**

- The teacher is familiar only with the state curriculum for reading and/or mathematics. **(Lacks Consistency with Model; 0 points)**

Action Plan
- The teacher addresses the assessment limit identified in the action plan during the first 5–7 minutes of the lesson. **(Reflects Exemplary Implementation of Model; 5 points)**
- The teacher addresses the assessment limit identified in the action plan at the beginning of the lesson for 7–10 minutes. **(Reflects Consistency with Model; 4 points)**
- The teacher addresses the assessment limit identified in the action plan at the beginning of the lesson for longer than 10 minutes. **(Lacks Consistency with Model; 3 points)**
- The teacher addresses the assessment limit identified in the action plan later in the lesson. **(Lacks Consistency with Model; 2 points)**
- The teacher does not address the assessment limit identified in the action plan during the lesson. **(Lacks Consistency with Model; 0 points)**

Reporting of Progress
- The teacher has a data center with a chart showing individual student/class performance on a pre-test and post-test on the identified assessment limits, and the chart is updated each week. **(Reflects Exemplary Implementation of Model; 5 points)**
- The teacher has a data center with a chart showing individual student/class performance on a pre-test and post-test on the identified assessment limits, and the chart is up to date, but some students are missing pre-test scores. **(Reflects Consistency with Model; 4 points)**
- The teacher has a data center with a chart showing individual student/class performance on a pre-test and post-test on the identified assessment limits, and the chart is up to date, but some students are missing post-test scores. **(Lacks Consistency with Model; 3 points)**
- The teacher has a data center with a chart showing individual student/class performance on a pre-test and post-test on the identified assessment limits, but it is not up to date. **(Lacks Consistency with Model; 2 points)**
- The teacher does not have a data center. **(Lacks Consistency with Model; 0 points)**

Lesson Objective

- The lesson objective is written in the "KNOW/DO" format; the "KNOW" is linked to the essential curriculum, and the "DO" requires higher order thinking. **(Reflects Exemplary Implementation of Model; 5 points)**
- The lesson objective is linked to the essential curriculum so the teacher can show other lessons with objectives in the "KNOW/DO" format, and the teacher can explain why this lesson is an exception (e.g., laboratory lesson, project, etc.). **(Reflects Consistency with Model; 4 points)**
- The lesson objective is not linked to the essential curriculum. **(Lacks Consistency with Model; 2 points)**
- The lesson objective is flawed. **(Lacks Consistency with Model; 0 points)**

Lesson Planning

- The teacher's lesson plans include some lessons in which the teacher explicitly teaches skills students are expected to master, and the plans illustrate how instruction is differentiated based on students' readiness, interests, and learning profile. **(Reflects Exemplary Implementation of Model; 5 points)**
- The teacher's lesson plans include some lessons in which the teacher explicitly teaches skills students are expected to master. **(Reflects Consistency with Model; 4 points)**
- The teacher's lesson plans do not include any explicit instructional lessons. **(Lacks Consistency with Model; 3 points)**
- The teacher's lesson plans do not indicate how the lesson is to be taught. **(Lacks Consistency with Model; 2 points)**
- The teacher does not have lesson plans. **(Lacks Consistency with Model; 0 points)**

5 Mastery of Assessment Limits	**Overall Scoring:**
4 Approaching Mastery	40 = Mastery,
3 Fair Progress	30 = Approaching Mastery
2 Lacking Progress	15 = Lacking Progress
0 Failing	Below 15 = Failing

REFERENCES

Baker, J. A. (1999). Teacher-student interaction in urban at-risk classrooms: Differential behavior, relationship quality, and student satisfaction with school. *The Elementary School Journal*, 100, 57–70.

Bloom, B. S. (1956). *Taxonomy of educational objectives, the classification of educational goals-handbook I Cognitive domain*. New York, NY: McKay.

Brown, K. E., & Medway, F. J. (2007). School climate and teacher beliefs in a school effectively serving poor South Carolina (USA) African American students: A case study. *Teaching and Teacher Education*, 23, 529–540.

Delpit, L. (2006). *Other people's children: Cultural conflict in the classroom*. New York, NY: The New Press.

Eisner, E. (1979). *The educational imagination: On the design and evaluation of school programs*. Upper Saddle River, NJ: Merrill Prentice Hall.

Fisher, E. J. (2005). Black student achievement and the oppositional culture model. *The Journal of Negro Education*, 74, 201–209.

Goddard, R. D., Hoy, W. K., & Hoy, A. W. (2000). Collective teacher efficacy: Its meaning, measure, and impact on student achievement. *American Educational Research Journal*, 37 (2), 479–507.

Hudley, C. A. (1997). Teacher practices and student motivation in a middle school program for African American males. *Urban Education, 32*, 304–319.

Maryland State Curriculum. Retrieved from http://mdk12. org/instruction/curriculum/index.html

Newmann, F. M., Bryk, A. S., & Nagoaka, J. K. (2001). *Authentic intellectual work and standardized tests: Conflict or coexistence? Improving Chicago's schools.* Chicago, IL: Consortium on Chicago School Research.

Patterson, K. B. (2005). Increasing outcomes for African American males in special education with the use of guided notes. *Journal of Negro Education, 74*, 311–320.

Quinn, M. M. (2002). Changing antisocial behavior patterns in young boys: A structured cooperative learning approach. *Education and Treatment of Children, 25*, 36.

Wilson, G. L., & Michaels, C. A. (2006). General and special education students' perceptions of co-teaching: Implications for secondary-level literacy instruction. *Reading and Writing Quarterly, 22*, 205–225.

INDEX

NOTE: Page numbers followed by f or t refer to figures or tables, respectively. Page numbers followed by tt refer to two relevant tables on a page.

A

Accommodations, instructional imperatives, 22t
Action Plan, 78–79t, 80–82, 119
Action Plan Calendar, 77, 83, 84–85t
Administrators and staff
  awareness of instructional imperative, 118
  components of Integrated Approach for, 28–33t
  role in addressing teacher expectations, 6, 7, 8
  support for culture of instruction, 13, 14f
  support for Integrated Approach Action Plan, 79t
Annual measurable outcomes, 35–36
  assessing prospects for meeting state requirements, 37–40
Assessment
  assessing prospects for meeting state requirements for school performance, 37–40
  biweekly, 27t
  frequency, 26t
  grading accuracy, 30t
  monthly reporting, 26t
  pre-tests and post-tests, 26t, 78–79t, 92
  progress charts and reports, 26t, 27t
  quarterly, 27t
  short cycle, 26t
  state requirements, 35–36, 43–44
  of student groups, 39–40, 41t
  student monitoring of, 87–88
  See also Assessment limits; Data Center Spreadsheet
Assessment limits
  action plan for teaching, 20t, 77, 84–85f, 119
  definition, 44, 117
  development, 44
  high school English, 55–58t
  for informational text comprehension, 48–49t, 51–52t, 84–85f
  for literary text comprehension, 49–51t, 53–54t
  mathematics (grades 3 to 8), 58–59, 59–75tt
  professional development for teaching, 82–83
  state requirements, 43–44
  in teaching practice, 44–47
  See also Data Center Spreadsheet

Authentic intellectual
  instruction, 16t
AYP (adequate yearly
  progress), 3, 19, 32, 35–36,
  38–40, 48, 128

B
Baker, J. A., 17t
Bloom, B. S., 16t, 98
Brown, K. E., 1–2
Byrk, A. S., 16t

C
Cognitive functioning
  characteristics of cultural
    groups, 11–12
  goals of education, 4–5,
    98–99
  higher order thinking, 16t
  instructional theory
    components in Integrated
Approach, 16t
  in learning process, 98
Cognitive pluralism
  as Integrated Approach
    component, 16t
  performance-based daily
    objectives, 99–105
  significance of, 97–98
Collective efficacy, 7
Cooperative learning, 17t, 109
Co-teaching, 17t, 29t
Culture of instruction
  absence of, 12
  assessing, 12–13
  characteristics of cultural
    groups, 11–12
  establishing, 13–14
  four elements of, 13, 14f

Integrated Approach
  Implementation Rubric, 118
  interaction of quadrants in,
    15f
  lesson planning in, 107
  student success in absence
    of, 13
  teacher expectations in, 7
Curriculum design
  essential skills, 21t
  knowledge of state
    requirements, 19t, 20t
  limitations in enhancing
    educational achievement,
    107
  teacher awareness of state
    requirements, 118–119

D
Data analysis
  assessing prospects for
    meeting state requirements
    for school performance,
    37–40
  components, 25–27
  in culture of instruction, 13,
    14f
Data Center Spreadsheet, 89t
  components, 89–90
  elementary schools, 90–91
  middle and high schools, 91
  monthly reporting charts, 92,
    93–95tt
  reports to faculty and staff, 92
  student access, 87–88
Delpit, L., 6
Disruptive students, 33t

E

Eisner, E., 16t
Elementary grades
Data Center Spreadsheet,
90–91
Integrated Approach Action
Plan, 80
mathematics assessment
limits, 59–65tt
reading assessment limits,
48–51t
English instruction
high school assessment limits,
55–58t
See also Reading
English language learners (ELL)
coded seating charts for
teachers, 25
exempt and not exempt, 37
instructional imperatives, 23t
professional development for
teachers, 113
teacher expectations of, 6, 117
weekend instruction, 30t

F

Federal mandates, 19, 43
Fisher, E. J., 18t

G

Goddard, R. D., 7
Grading, accuracy of, 30t
Group assessments, 39–40, 41t
Guided notes, 18t

H

Hall passes, 24t
Higher order thinking, 16t
High school
Data Center Spreadsheet, 91

English assessment limits,
55–58t
Integrated Approach Action
Plan, 82
Homework
grading accuracy, 30t
late policy, 29t
Hoy, A. W., 7
Hoy, W. K., 7
Hudley, C. A., 17t

I

Informal Observation Checklist,
115–116
Instructional imperatives
components, 19–24t
in culture of instruction, 13,
14f
Instructional theory
components, 16–18t
in culture of instruction, 13,
14f
Integrated Approach
Action Plan, 78–79t, 80–82
Action Plan Calendar, 83,
84–85t
administrative support
components, 28–33t
data analysis in, 25–27
Data Center Spreadsheet,
87–90
Implementation Rubric, 117
Informal Observation
Checklist, 115–116
instructional imperatives,
19–24t
instructional theory
components, 16–18f
Lesson Plan, 21t, 107–111,
120

professional development,
28t, 113–114
Projection Template, 37
Interruptions during
instruction, 24t

L
Lesson Plan, 21t, 107–111, 120

M
Manipulatives, in math instruction, 23t
Mathematics instruction
assessing prospects for
meeting state requirements,
37–39
assessment limits, 58–59,
59–75tt
Data Center Spreadsheet, 90,
91
elementary school action plan,
80
high school action plan, 82
middle school action plan, 81
performance-based objectives,
100
use of manipulatives, 23t
Medway, F. J., 1–2
Michaels, C. A., 17t
Middle grades
Data Center Spreadsheet, 91
Integrated Approach Action
Plan, 81
mathematics assessment
limits, 65–73tt
reading assessment limits,
51–54t
sample Action Plan Calendar,
84–85f

N
Nagoaka, J. K., 16t
Newmann, F. M., 16t

P
Paraprofessionals, 32t
Parents of low-performing
students, meeting with, 25t
Patterson, K. B., 18t
Performance-based objectives
applicable subjects, 100
cognitive functioning, 99–105
instructional imperatives, 20t
Integrated Approach
Implementation Rubric, 120
Planning
Action Plan Calendar, 77, 83,
84–85t
co-planning, 29t
importance of, 2–3, 3–4
instructional imperatives in
Integrated Approach, 21t
Integrated Approach Action
Plan, 78–79t, 80–83, 84–85t
Integrated Approach Lesson
Plan Format, 21t, 107–111,
120
manifestations of teacher
expectations, 2
teacher daily plan, 33t
Professional development, 28t,
82–83, 113–114
Progress charts and reports, 26t,
27t

Q
Quinn, M. M., 17t

R

Race/ethnicity, group assessments, 39

Reading
assessing prospects for meeting state requirements, 37–39
Data Center Spreadsheet, 90, 91
elementary school action plan, 80
high school action plan, 82
informational text comprehension, 43–44, 47, 48–49t, 51–52t, 84–85f
instructional assistants, 32t
literary text comprehension, 43–44, 47, 49–51t, 53–54t
middle school action plan, 81
Middle School Action Plan Calendar, 84–85f
performance-based cognitive pluralism objectives, 100–105
state requirements for curriculum and performance, 43–45
word parts analysis, 45–47

Reflective teachers, 5–6, 111

Related Arts instruction, 79t, 80, 90, 91

Reteaching, 22t

Rigor, 4–5

Rote memory tasks, 4, 97–98

S

Saturday academy, 30t

Seating charts, 25t

Self-expectation, effect of teacher expectations on students', 1–2

Site-based administrative team. *See* Administrators and staff

Small group instruction, 17t

Special education teachers as content experts, 31t

State requirements
assessing school prospects for meeting, 37–40
instructional imperatives in Integrated Approach, 19–20t
Integrated Approach Implementation Rubric, 118–119
reading, 43–44
scope, 43

Student achievement
coded seating charts for teachers, 25t
cognitive goals, 4–5, 98–99
culture of instruction for, 13, 107
meetings with parents of low-performing students, 25t
mitigating ineffective teaching, 2
performance-based daily objectives, 99–105
progress charts, 26t
significance of teacher expectations in, 1–2, 3, 5
strategy for, 3–4
student monitoring of, 87–88
success in absence of culture of instruction, 13
See also Assessment

SWBAT (students will be able to), 100–105

T

Teacher expectations
    action template, 9t
    assessing, 6, 8, 9t
    in culture of instruction, 7
    harmful effects of low
        expectations, 6–7
    in Integrated Approach, 7, 18t
    Integrated Approach
        Implementation Rubric, 117
    manifestations, 2
    school administrators' role in
        addressing, 6, 7
    significance of, in student
        performance, 1–2, 3, 5, 6
    theory of peak performance,
        8f
Teaching practice
    administrative support, 28–33t
    instructional assistants, 32t
    instructional imperatives in
        Integrated Approach, 20–24t
    instructional theory
        components in Integrated
        Approach, 17–18t
    manifestations of teacher
        expectations, 2
    minimizing interruptions, 24t
    needs-specific seminar
        courses, 27t
    performance evaluation, 28t
    professional development,
        28t, 82–83, 113–114
    reflective, 5–6
    rote memory tasks, 4
    use of assessment limits,
        44–47, 77
    See also Integrated Approach;
        Planning; Teacher
        expectations

V

Vocabulary, 19t
    functional requirements, 46
    word parts analysis, 45–47

W

Wilson, G. L., 17t
Word parts analysis, 45–47
Writing, instructional
    imperatives, 22t

ABOUT THE AUTHOR

 A former elementary teacher and high school teacher of English literature, Donyall D. Dickey is currently a Howard County, Maryland, middle school principal; a Johns Hopkins University graduate school instructor; an author; and sought-after educational consultant. He is a graduate of the University of Texas at Austin, Loyola University—where he earned a Master of Education in Administration & Supervision and is currently a doctoral candidate at George Washington University in Educational Leadership & Policy studies, researching student achievement and standards-based assessments.

Dickey's career is characterized by promoting unparalleled student achievement and school improvement. Each of the three schools where he has served as a school administrator has demonstrated record gains on state assessments. Most recently, he has led a previously underperforming middle school to unmatched gains on state and local assessments, transforming it into a model for instructional leadership for the region and the nation. Student groups—regardless of race/ethnicity, special needs, socioeconomic status, or English proficiency—demonstrated double-digit gains in just one year using this model. Other schools implementing his coaching method have consistently demonstrated similar gains.

Dickey is recognized as an authority on curriculum and instruction, as well as the administration of schools. His ideas for closing the achievement gap are used in schools across the nation, making the goal of adequate yearly progress possible for thousands of children who experience his methods.

For more information—or for Donyall Dickey's national training schedule of on-site professional development:

- Visit www.educationalepiphany.com
- E-mail donyall.dickey@educationalepiphany.com
- Contact the publisher at www.ahaprocess.com or (800) 424-9484